ALSO BY

Edward S. Corwin

National Supremacy: Treaty Power vs. State Power
(1913)
The Doctrine of Judicial Review: Its Legal and
Historical Basis, and Other Essays
(1914)
The French Policy and the American Alliance of
1778 (1916)
The President's Control of Foreign Relations
(1917)
John Marshall and the Constitution (1919)
The Constitution and What It Means Today
(1920, 1946)
The President's Removal Power under the Con-
stitution (1927)
The Democratic Dogma and Other Essays (1929)
The Twilight of the Supreme Court: A History of
Our Constitutional Theory (1934)
The Commerce Power versus States Rights (1936)
Court over Constitution (1938)
Constitutional Revolution, Ltd. (1941, 1946)
The President: Office and Powers (1940, 1941)
The Constitution and World Organization (1944)

Total War and the Constitution

THE WILLIAM W. COOK FOUNDATION *was established at the University of Michigan to endow a distinguished Lectureship on American Institutions. The donor, William Wilson Cook, long a member of the New York bar, received the degree of Bachelor of Arts from the College of Literature, Science, and the Arts of the University in 1880, and the degree of Bachelor of Laws from the Law School in 1882. The lectures presented in this volume are the second in the series of lectures under the Foundation. They were delivered in the Rackham lecture halls at the University in March 1946, and are published, under a special arrangement between the University and the publisher, as the second volume in the lectureship series. The first volume was* Freedom and Responsibility in the American Way of Life, *by Carl L. Becker.*

TOTAL WAR

AND THE

CONSTITUTION

Five lectures delivered on the William W. Cook Foundation
at the University of Michigan, March 1946

By EDWARD S. CORWIN

With an Introduction by E. BLYTHE STASON
Dean, University of Michigan Law School

New York   *ALFRED A. KNOPF*   1947

FIRST EDITION

FOR
Alma Mater

Introduction

By E. BLYTHE STASON

TOTAL WAR AND THE CONSTITUTION is a written record of
constitutional interpretation in one of the most difficult
periods in American history. First delivered as a series of
lectures under the auspices of the William W. Cook Foundation at the University of Michigan and now published
in this volume, the monograph is a carefully reasoned record of recent trends in constitutional theory, and, in addition, it is a repository of a wealth of factual information
concerning the maneuvers of the years immediately prior
to and during World War II, resulting in the shift in constitutional dominance over the affairs of the nation from
the legislative and judicial supremacy of bygone years to
the ascendancy of the executive branch of government.
Written by a master of constitutional history, government,
and political theory, the volume is an authoritative interpretation of events of paramount contemporary interest.

It is not seemly for a foreword to foretell the author's
story. But the summarization in Professor Corwin's final
lecture on the "Postwar Constitution" calls forth one important and unanswered question. Is the proper balance
being maintained between the forces demanding change
and those representing the desire for reasonable stability in
national affairs? Or is current constitutional interpretation
proceeding with undue haste to scrap tried and still useful
landmarks?

The question is, of course, unanswerable except by way
of general speculation, but no thinking person can study
recent regulatory legislation without wondering about the
matter — without asking himself, for example, how far we
can continue to progress in the direction of conferring

upon administrative officials more and more virtually un-reviewable discretionary power over the lives and activities of men without finally reaching a state of absolutism that can no longer be called a liberal democracy. To offer but a single illustration of the trend, the very latest Congressional venture in administrative legislation is most revealing. I refer to the so-called Atomic Energy Act adopted in June 1946, creating the Atomic Energy Commission and giving it plenary powers over the production and use of fissionable materials. Although the history of recent years reveals many instances of somewhat similar, but less sweeping delegation of discretionary regulatory powers, no other peacetime enactment of anything like the importance of the Atomic Energy Act has conferred upon an administrative agency anything like so much uncanalized discretionary power over an important phase of American life. Conceding the necessity in this as in many other instances, nevertheless, we are confronted by the uncomfortable fact that the experience of history has not yet shown us how constitutional democratic institutions can be preserved in the presence and under the control of ever increasing administrative discretion. The solution is one of the prime tasks posed for the future — a challenge to the scientific world.

In two successive years the lectures on the William W. Cook Foundation have furnished substance for careful and reflective attention on the part of all who are interested in constitutional democracy. In 1945 the late Professor Carl L. Becker delivered his lectures entitled *Freedom and Responsibility in the American Way of Life,* presenting therein the wisdom derived from a lifetime of scholarship as a historian in the American scene. In 1946 Professor Corwin gives us *Total War and the Constitution,* which, by its constructive comment upon current trends in constitutional theory, broadens and enriches our understanding of the

American institution that is our fundamental law. It is impossible that too much of such thought-provoking comment be made accessible if American institutions are to serve their best in a scientific but bewildered and thoroughly chaotic world.

Ann Arbor, Michigan
October 15, 1946

Preface

A PREFACE is a kind of last call to dinner. It affords the author his last clear chance to say something that should have been said earlier and to make appropriate acknowledgments. I am availing myself of the present opportunity for both purposes.

The tangency of the Nuremberg trials — that is to say, of American participation in them — with the Constitution is so slight that I have dealt with the subject in a footnote, to which I wish here to add a supplementary word or two. Many defenders of the trials resent the contention that the punishment of Göring and his associates violated the maxim *"nulla poena sine lege"* and our own Constitution's condemnation of *ex post facto* laws. Dealing with this objection in its verdict, the Nuremberg Court describes *"ex post facto* legislation" as "abhorrent to all civilized nations," but adds quite inconsequently: "the Tribunal has been concerned with matters of substance and not mere procedure"! Perhaps the Court had in mind the distinction between *legislation* and *adjudication,* for, as Bentham pointed out, the latter is characteristically retroactive — like "beating a dog for what he has done." This is clearly Justice Jackson's position in his opening statement as Prosecutor, when he remarks: "The fact is that when the law evolves by the case method . . . it advances at the expense of those who wrongly guessed the law and learned too late their error." The answer is, of course, that the Constitution intended to rule out this element of retroactivity in the devising and imposition of *penalties.* Justice Jackson was rather more forthright when he remarked on the same occasion: "If there is no law under which to try these people, it is about time the human race made some."

Preface

Throughout the entire discussion of the merits of the Nuremberg verdict one curious but very pertinent fact seems to have been forgotten, and I am much indebted to my friend Charles Howard McIlwain for bringing it to my attention. This is the fact that as far back as 1935 the Nazis themselves had given their enthusiastic endorsement to the idea of *ex post facto* penalties. I quote from a dispatch of July 5, 1935 from the Berlin correspondent of the London *Times:*

> A principle entirely new to German jurisprudence has been introduced by the Penal Code Amendment Law, which was one of the batch of laws published by the Reich Cabinet on June 26 and is promulgated today in the official *Gazette.* It is that the Courts shall punish offences not punishable under the code when they are deserving of punishment "according to the underlying idea of a penal code or according to healthy public sentiment *(Volksempfinden)*." If no penal code applies directly, such an offence is to be punished according to that law the underlying idea of which best fits it . . . (McIlwain: *Constitutionalism and the Changing World,* p. 268).

The dispatch also notes that Dr. Hans Frank, "former Reich Commissar for Justice," "declares the new law to be a landmark on the road to a National Socialist penal code."

Dr. Frank was one of the ten men executed two weeks ago — "hoist," one may possibly be permitted to remark, "by his own petard"!

I gave these lectures last March 18 to 22, inclusive. For the kindnesses and courtesies extended to me in the course of those five days by Dean Stason and other representatives of the University of Michigan and by friends and relatives I find it impossible to make adequate acknowledgment in this place. Suffice it to say, I don't see how I could have been better treated or given a pleasanter time.

I wish to thank Professor McIlwain for assistance in reading proof, Mr. Milton Rugoff for his practiced patience with authors, and Alma Fell for her efficient work as typist.

EDWARD S. CORWIN

Princeton, New Jersey
October 29, 1946

Contents

Total War and the Constitution

WE MAY *well wonder in view of the precedents now estab-*
lished whether constitutional government as hitherto main-
tained in this Republic could survive another great war even
victoriously waged.

THE HONORABLE CHARLES EVANS HUGHES

June 21, 1920

I

The War Before the War

WHEN most people encounter the expression "total war" they think of an aggressor pursuing ends that take no account the rights of others, by means equally ruthless. While the phrase itself is of recent coinage, total war in this primary sense is at least as old as recorded history and enjoys, at times, the most exalted sanction. In Deuteronomy xx we read:

> Of the cities of these people, which the Lord thy God doth give thee for an inheritance, thou shalt save alive nothing that breatheth: But thou shalt utterly destroy them; namely, the Hittites, and the Amorites, the Canaanites, and the Perizzites, the Hivites, and the Jebusites; as the Lord thy God hath commanded thee.

The character of the justification that was supposed to underlie this policy of ruthlessness is interesting too:

> For thou art an holy people unto the Lord thy God: the Lord thy God hath chosen thee to be a special people unto himself, above all people that are upon the face of the earth.[1]

Anglo-American policy toward the Indians stemmed from a similar motivation and a similar objective. Many years ago I had occasion to go through the statute books of the early American colonies. In Volume I of Hening's *Virginia Statutes* I came upon this entry:

> March 5, 1623–4. . . . That at the beginning of July next the inhabitants of every corporation shall fall upon their adjoyning salvages as we did the last year.[2]

---

1 Deuteronomy vii, 6.
2 Hening: *Statutes at Large*, I, 128 (1823).

3

In this brisk enactment are summarized the essential characteristics of British-American Indian policy from start to finish — that is to say, the finish of the Indians as a power capable of disputing our appropriation of the North American continent. At the same time our none too sensitive forebears salved their consciences by courting the belief that the Indians were an inferior race, supposing indeed they really were human. British-American conquest of North America thus bore many resemblances to the Nazi conquest of Poland, only the latter, thanks to modern science, was of course vastly more speedy and more efficient. And Spanish conquest of the southern portion of the American continent, although less systematically prosecuted than that by our ancestors of the northern portion, frequently paralleled it in fortuitous violence, as is illustrated in Humboldt's allusion to a South American tribe which was so completely wiped out by its Spanish conquerors that "only a parrot was left to perpetuate the idiom of the race" — a feat that, to judge from the usual preferences of parrots in such matters, was no service to the memory of either the idiom or the race.

Totality of objective and method is of only passing interest in the present connection, however, for while it has given international law as it previously existed the *coup de grâce*, its traceable influence on constitutional law, at least prior to the Nuremberg trials, has been too indirect to be assessable. The totality we are interested in is "functional totality," by which I mean the politically ordered participation in the war effort of all personal and social forces, the scientific, the mechanical, the commercial, the economic, the moral, the literary and artistic, and the psychological. This is the aspect of total war that is of directest relevance to a study of the impact of war on the Constitution, and not solely in this war but also in lesser measure in those earlier more or less total wars, World War I and the Civil War.

When did "functional totality" make its first appearance as idea if not as fact? I am disposed to answer by pointing to the proclamation of the Committee of Public Safety to the people of France at the beginning of the War of 1793:

> The young men will go to battle; married men will forge arms and transport food; the women will make tents, garments, and help in the hospitals; the children will cut old rags into strips; the old men will place themselves in the public square to inflame the courage of the warriors, incite hatred against the Kings, and recommend the unity of the Republic.[3]

The picture we have here is of a society every human element of which is involved in the struggle. But more than that, this document signalizes in the *levée en masse* the appearance of the conscript army, which is one of the *two* efficient causes of total war in the functional sense. Following the decline of the feudal array after Agincourt in 1415, European armies gradually became volunteer, mercenary, and professional. They were also, by modern standards, small armies; and the social consequences of their creation and maintenance were correspondingly slight. Very different was it with the conscript army from the outset. The creation of such a force marked a tremendous accession to the conceded powers of government; the forced withdrawal of such great numbers from the normal pursuits of daily life disturbed the social economy profoundly, while the task that was put upon the depleted society of supplying and equipping such numbers aggravated the disturbance. Finally, as the Committee of Public Safety was alert to perceive, a conscript army poses a problem of *morale* not only

---

[3] Quoted in Edward Mead Earle (editor) : *Modern Strategy* (Princeton, 1944) , p. 77. On the invasion of Ethiopia by the Fascists early in 1935, the King of Kings issued the following order: "All married men from 14 to 80 report, bringing weapons. Married men bring wives to cook and work. Single men bring any convenient woman. Men found at home will be shot."

as respects the army itself, but also as respects society at large.

The conception of war that the French Revolution imposed upon the world through the *levée en masse* has been *today amplified and extended by science and invention — by technology,* in a word; and whereas the key word of total war was once *personnel,* today it is *personnel* and *matériel,* with the latter at times manifesting an almost moral preponderance. The two things cannot of course really be separated. Napoleon's epigram that "God is always on the side of the heaviest artillery" may have expressed an attitude that was more deferential toward matériel than toward Deity, but it nevertheless pointed down the road that warfare was to take till August 6, 1945. In the recent war we were informed variously that it took ten, fifteen, twenty, even forty men on the ground to service a single bomber, which, whether it spells the subordination of personnel to matériel or not, certainly symbolizes the stress and strain that total war, because of its requirements of both of these, puts upon society, government, and the Constitution.

2

The question inevitably, if somewhat prematurely, suggests itself of how the atomic bomb will be likely to affect the impact of total war on the Constitution. The strategy that will stem from that horrendous discovery has still to be elaborated, but a few remarks may be ventured without too great an appearance of rashness. I assume that the principal cause of war, aside from sheer desperation on the part of the attacking party, or the motive of revenge — which, to be sure, may play a considerable role in the future [4] — is

4 "The exhaustion of defeat does not itself bring mental conversion; it is more likely to bring increased desire for revenge, since every misfortune can be attributed to the malevolence of the conqueror. Thus, while the victors may be led to believe that owing to their victory there will be no more

the expectation of the attacking party that he will be successful. I assume too that for an indefinite time the principal guarantee against the use of the atomic bomb by one state against another must be the likelihood that the party subjected to attack will still be able to retaliate in kind; and I agree with Mr. Bernard Brodie that "the political facts of life concerning the United States Government under its present Constitution make it highly likely that, if war comes, we will receive the first blow rather than deliver it." And from these premises it seems a sound conclusion that "our most urgent military problem is," as Mr. Brodie puts it, "to organize ourselves to survive a vastly more destructive 'Pearl Harbor' than occurred in 1941. Otherwise we shall not be able to take the offensive at all." [5]

In other words, we must do those things which will guarantee that whatever happens we shall still retain the power of retaliation. *What is more, all other nations must perceive that we do retain it.* What measures this prescription will entail it is unnecessary for us to speculate upon at any length. The armed forces must certainly be kept in condition to prevent a bomb attack from being followed up by an invasion. Doubtless our industrial centers will have to be more widely dispersed.[6] Nor, as Mr. Brodie points out, will it be safe to keep

---

war, the losers may be confirmed, paradoxically, in their philosophy of aggression by the consequences of defeat. . . . It is perhaps worth noticing that during the last century and a quarter the reaction of the defeated party has tended to come a little sooner after each of three great wars." E. L. Woodward in the *New York Times*, Magazine Section, June 16, 1946.

[5] *The Atomic Bomb and American Security,* Yale Institute of International Studies, Memorandum No. 18 (November 1, 1945) , p. 9. For a highly skeptical estimate of the feasibility of effective international control of the atomic bomb, see E. L. Woodward: *Some Political Consequences of the Atomic Bomb* (Pamphlet, Oxford University Press, 1946) . Both studies have since been published as chapters in *The Absolute Weapon; Atomic Power and World Order* by Frederick S. Dunn and others (New York, 1946) .

[6] The Winter Park conference on the atomic bomb voiced some very

concentrated in a single city not only the main agencies of National Government but also the whole Executive branch, including the several successors to the Presidency. While an aggressor could hardly count upon destroying at one blow all the persons who might assume leadership in a crisis, he might, unless there were considerably greater geographic decentralization of national leadership than exists at present, do enough damage with one bomb to create complete confusion in the mobilization of resistance.[7]

This is undoubtedly a thought that the Senate Judiciary Committee, of which a subcommittee is at present engaged in recasting the Presidential Succession Act, ought to take into account.

Thus the atomic bomb is likely, if we take its menace with proper seriousness, to have considerable effect upon both our industrial and our constitutional structure. But now note that *the effect will not be confined to wartime* (wars waged with atomic bombs are likely to be over in a few hours), *but will be spread through peacetime. The effects of the impact of total war on the Constitution will thus become embedded in the peacetime Constitution.* This is especially true of the effects on governmental set-up,

---

gloomy conclusions as to the possibility of an effective dispersal of industry and on some other points. The following is an extract from a dispatch to the *New York Times* of March 12, 1946, concerning the conference:

"In answer to a question about the advisability of dispersing our industries to make them less vulnerable to atomic bomb attacks, Professor Rabi, Nobel laureate in physics, said that dispersal would not make any difference as industrial plants must remain in the neighborhood of their raw materials, within an area that could be destroyed by a concentrated attack with atomic bombs. An attack with 10,000 bombs, he said, would destroy all England and an area the size of Indiana and Illinois.

"Professor Smyth said that an estimate of the cost of decentralization indicated that it would be $250,000,000,000 to $300,000,000,000."

Russia's achievement in removing her industries in front of the advancing Nazi forces, however, throws a more hopeful light on the suggestion.

[7] Brodie, op. cit., in note 5 above.

8

but there may be serious results for private rights too. I fall back again upon Mr. Brodie:

> The engine necessary for utilizing the explosive, that is, the bomb itself, seems from various hints contained in the *Smyth Report* to be a highly intricate and fairly massive mechanism. But it is also probable that a nation intent upon perfecting the atomic bomb as a sabotage instrument could work out a much simpler device, something which permitted the major part of the materials used to be gathered and prepared locally in the target area.
>
> At any rate, the war of the future might very well take the form of a revelation by one nation to another that the latter's major cities had atomic bombs planted in them and that only immediate and absolute submission to dictate [*sic*] would prevent them from going off. . . . Under such conditions an extraordinarily high premium is attached to national competence in sabotage on the one hand and in counter-sabotage work on the other. To a community alerted to national danger the F.B.I. or its counterpart becomes the first line of defense, and the encroachment on civil liberties which would necessarily follow would far exceed in magnitude and pervasiveness anything which democracies have thus far tolerated in peacetime.[8]

It should be added that the extension to the United States of a really thoroughgoing system of international inspection aimed to keep the atomic bomb under the control of the United Nations would have a like effect.

Little wonder that some of our nuclear scientists are consternated by their own handicraft! Their attempt, nevertheless, to prove that the atomic bomb, just because of its destructive force, has made war "impossible" is hardly persuasive, any more than was the assurance of the bus-driver to his nervous passengers that he *couldn't* drive over the precipice that their road ran beside, "because," said he, "if we drove over that we'd all be killed!" The atomic bomb may have effectively prevented all future wars *except* the

[8] Ibid.

next one, but that is just the war that today has mankind so deeply, so justifiably troubled.[9]

3

American participation in World War II proceeded through two stages — before and after Pearl Harbor. In the first stage, with which this lecture deals, the country, abandoning the status of "neutral" for that of "non-belliger-

[9] "Past feelings about 'new' weapons can seem comic to us now. There was a Spartan hero, Archidamus, four centuries before Christ, who saw a soldier killed at a range of some hundreds of yards by a projectile from a wooden catapult. 'Oh Hercules!' he groaned, 'the valour of man is at an end!' Don Quixote complained, at the beginning of another 'cycle' in the development of projectile weapons, that gunpowder could cause . . . 'a cowardly base hand to take away the life of the bravest gentleman . . . a chance bullet (shot perhaps by one that fled, and was frightened at the very flash the mischievous piece gave when it went off) coming nobody knows how or from whence, puts a period to the brave designs and the life of one that deserved to have survived many years. . . .' Feudal chivalry feeling, like other social forces before and after it, that it had the right to be eternal, loathed the new weapon that was to level it. It tried to outlaw the musket. It executed musketeers taken prisoner; that was the practice even of the Chevalier Bayard, whose name has become our symbol for chivalrous magnanimity. As late as 1676 the terrible accusation was being made that gunners were irreligious, almost infidels. In that year an English writer began his 'light on the Art of Gunnery' with the words: 'The reason, wherefore my first discourse is of Gunners, is only because many times it falleth out, that most men employed for Gunners, are very negligent of the fear of God.' How many times have we heard that sentiment echoed, since Hiroshima, about 'the scientists'?

"Nobel, remembered for his Peace Prizes (still optimistically awarded at intervals) and for the invention of dynamite, considered that his inventions would do more than his Prizes for the cause of peace: high explosive would make war so horrible that civilized nations would renounce it. He was right; they have renounced it quite often. But as they do not take the necessary steps to make renunciation effective, war recurs. A belief like that held by Nobel has animated various innovators at various times; it has never been justified and does not seem to be justified in regard to the atom bomb today." Tom Wintringham: "The Last Weapon," *Virginia Quarterly Review*, Spring 1946, pp. 198–9.

Mr. Wintringham makes a persuasive argument to show that it was fear of retaliation that kept the principal powers from using poison gas against each other in World War II.

ent," became, under the late President Roosevelt's stimulation, the "arsenal of democracy." Throughout the period Presidential power in the field of foreign relations, which stems primarily from the opening clause of Article II of the Constitution, was brought into full requisition, and was importantly supplemented by other powers to which Mr. Roosevelt laid claim as "Commander-in-Chief." The period reached its culmination on the home front in the enactment of Lend-Lease and on the diplomatic front in a "shooting war" in the effort that ensued upon Lend-Lease to get supplies to our British friends through the German submarine cordon.

The opening clause of Article II of the Constitution reads: "The Executive power shall be vested in a President of the United States of America." This is the final form of a proposal that as adopted by the Convention read: "The Executive power of the United States shall be vested in a single person. His style shall be 'President of the United States of America.' His title shall be 'His Excellency' " — words that were designed to settle the issue whether the Executive should be collegiate or single and, incidentally, to name the office. The final form came from the pen of Gouverneur Morris, who headed the Convention's Committee of Style, and was never separately acted on by the Convention. Its terse elegance, characteristic of "the hand that wrote the Constitution," incorporates a fundamental ambiguity, and not improbably a calculated one. Is the clause still a simple designation of office, or is it the fountain-head of all the President's powers?

In the first debate in Congress under the Constitution the latter view was urged by Madison among others and materially influenced the ascription to the President of the power to remove his principal subordinates. And four years later the same doctrine was appealed to by Hamilton in his famous "Letters of Pacificus," which were written in defense of Washington's Proclamation of Neutrality on the outbreak of war between France and Great Britain. This time Madison, over the *nom de guerre* "Helvidius," espoused the other side of the question. "Helvidius" charged "Pacificus" with endeavoring brazenly to import into the "executive power" clause the prerogative of the British Crown in the conduct of diplomatic relations, a doctrine which he endeavored to rebut by pointing out that whereas the prerogative of the British crown embraced the power to declare war, this power was specifically vested by the Constitution in Congress. It followed, Madison urged, that Congress, not the President, had the sole power to determine all issues of war and peace, and hence the issue of neutrality. Indeed, it was "Helvidius'" contention that the President's powers in the field of foreign relations were meant to be little more than instrumental, that major policy-making in this field was the exclusive prerogative of Congress.[10]

"Helvidius" prosecuted his argument with immense acuity, but history has awarded the palm of victory to "Pacificus." *Immeasurably the greatest single force in setting the course of American foreign policy has been Presidential initiative,* and for reasons that had been earlier pointed out by Jay in *Federalist* 64. Only in the office of President are to be found those qualities of unity, energy, superior access to pertinent information, and the ability to act swiftly and secretly which answer to the protean nature of international relations and their ever present tendency to slide into some unanticipated condition of crisis. By his reading of the "executive power" clause "Pacificus" gave the President constitutional warrant to go ahead and apply the advantages of his position in a field of power to which they are especially adapted.

[10] For substantially the full text of this debate, see my *President's Control of Foreign Relations* (Princeton, 1917), pp. 7–27.

One concession, it is true, Hamilton himself was prepared to make to the champions of Congressional power. Asserting "the right of the Executive, in certain cases, to determine the conduct of the nation, though it may, in its consequences, affect the exercise of the power of the legislature to declare war," he continued:

> Nevertheless, the executive cannot thereby control the exercise of that power. The legislature is still free to perform its duties, according to its own sense of them; though the executive, in the exercise of its constitutional powers, may establish an antecedent state of things, which ought to weigh in the legislative decision. The division of the executive power in the Constitution creates a *concurrent* authority in the cases to which it relates.

Hamilton here states a sound constitutional principle that is today incontestable, although he himself was to contradict it three years later when he advised Washington that the House of Representatives was under a *constitutional* as well as an *international* obligation to vote the funds that were necessary for carrying the recently ratified Jay Treaty into effect. I refer to the principle that Congress always remains a free agent in the exercise of its constitutional powers whatever any other organ or organs of government may have previously done in the exercise of theirs. The record of events proves, to be sure, that this theoretical freedom is often *practically* a snare and delusion, and in regard to nothing so much as the very power that "Pacificus" specifically mentions, that of declaring war. Our three wars of outstanding importance prior to World War II were all the direct outcome of Presidential policies in the making of which Congress had but a minor part. Our entrance into World War II, it is true, diverges from this pattern somewhat. For this was a long-drawn-out affair, marked by many seeming retreats, which nevertheless always put us a step nearer the final denouement, and it was terminated by the enemy pulling us into the maelstrom instead of our leaping into it. None the less, the initiative throughout was unremittingly with the President, and the story as a whole only emphasizes the essential truth of "Helvidius'" contention that "Pacificus'" reading of the "executive power" clause contravened, certainly in effect, the express intention of the Constitution that the war-declaring power should lodge with the legislative authority.

We turn now to the "Commander-in-Chief" clause: "The President shall be the Commander-in-Chief of the Army and Navy of the United States, and of the Militia of the several States, when called into the actual service of the United States." Commenting in *Federalist* 69 on this provision, Hamilton wrote:

> In this respect his authority would be nominally the same with that of the King of Great Britain, but in substance much inferior to it. It would amount to nothing more than the supreme command and direction of the military and naval forces, as first General and Admiral of the Confederacy; while that of the British King extends to the *declaring* of war and to the *raising* and *regulating* of fleets and armies, — all which, by the Constitution under consideration, would appertain to the legislature.

Rendered freely, this appears to mean that in any war in which the United States becomes involved — one presumably declared by Congress — the President will be top general and top admiral of the forces provided by Congress, so that no one can be put over him or be authorized to give him orders in the direction of the said forces. But otherwise he will have no powers that any high military or naval commander who was not also President might not have. Additional testimony as to the purely military significance originally attached to the clause is afforded by Story's statement in his *Commentaries,* written nearly half a century later, that the only objection leveled against it

14

in the States' ratifying conventions was that "it would be dangerous to let him [the President] command in person." "The propriety," Story adds, "of admitting the President to be Commander-in-Chief, so far as to give orders and have a general superintendency, was admitted." [11]

And that the clause was still in 1850 the forgotten clause of the Constitution is shown by Chief Justice Taney's opinion in *Fleming* v. *Page*,[12] in which, in holding that the military occupancy of the port of Tampico in the course of the Mexican War by the order of the President did not annex that place to the United States, the Chief Justice, speaking for the unanimous Court, said:

> His [the President's] duty and his power are purely military. As commander-in-chief, he is authorized to direct the movements of the naval and military forces placed by law at his command, and to employ them in the manner he may deem most effectual to harass and conquer and subdue the enemy. He may invade the hostile country, and subject it to the sovereignty and authority of the United States. But his conquests do not enlarge the boundaries of this Union, nor extend the operation of our institutions and laws beyond the limits before assigned to them by the legislative power. . . .
>
> In the distribution of political power between the great departments of government, there is such a wide difference between the power conferred on the President of the United States, and the authority and sovereignty which belong to the English crown, that it would be altogether unsafe to reason from any supposed resemblance between them, either as regards conquest in war, or any other subject where the rights and powers of the executive arm of the government are brought into question.

This static conception of the clause throughout the first seventy years of our history requires, nevertheless, to be amended in two respects. By the Act of 1807 Congress itself

---

[11] *Commentaries*, § 1492.
[12] 9 How. 603.

empowered the President to employ the armed forces of the United States "to execute the laws, suppress insurrections, and repel invasions," the same purposes for which he had been earlier authorized to employ the militia of the several States; and without the sanction of Congress successive Presidents had from the time of Jefferson utilized contingents of both the Army and the Navy, although much more commonly the latter, for the protection of the rights of American citizens abroad and even in the prosecution of vaguer national interests — as an arm, in short, of his power in the field of foreign relations.[13]

4

The sudden emergence of the "Commander-in-Chief" clause as one of the most highly charged provisions of the Constitution occurred almost overnight in consequence of Lincoln's wedding it to the clause that makes it the duty of the President "to take care that the laws be faithfully executed." From these two clauses thus united Lincoln proceeded to derive what he termed the "war power," to justify the series of extraordinary measures that he took in the interval between the fall of Fort Sumter and the convening of Congress in special session on July 4, 1861. During this period of ten weeks Lincoln embodied the State militias into a volunteer army of 300,000 men, added 23,000 men to the Regular Army and 18,000 to the Navy, paid out two millions from unappropriated funds in the Treasury to persons unauthorized to receive it, closed the Post Office to "treasonable correspondence," subjected passengers to and from foreign countries to new passport regulations, proclaimed a blockade of the Southern ports, suspended the writ of habeas corpus in various places, caused the arrest and military detention of persons "who were represented to him" as being engaged in or contemplating "trea-

[13] This matter is discussed at some length in Lecture IV.

sonable practices" — and all this for the most part without
the least statutory authorization.[14]

In his Message of July 4 Lincoln expressed the opinion
that his blockade declaration and his call for militia had
been "strictly legal"; also the hope that Congress would
"readily ratify" his enlargement of the Army and Navy,
which Congress did a month later. As to his action respecting habeas corpus the President advanced two lines of reasoning. One of these, including his famous question: "Are
all the laws *but one* to go unexecuted, and the Government
itself go to pieces lest that one be violated?" logically implies that the President may, in an emergency thought by
him to require it, partially suspend the Constitution. In
the second place, he argued, the framers could not have intended to leave the power of suspending the habeas corpus
privilege solely to Congress, since that would mean "that
in every case the danger should run its course until Congress could be called together, the very assembling of which
might be prevented, as was intended in this case." Nevertheless, he was content, he said, to leave "the subject entirely to the better judgment of Congress," which by doing
nothing left the President's action undisturbed and so in
effect conceded his power to take it, an inference that was
confirmed eighteen months later by the terms of the Act of
March 3, 1863. His remaining extraordinary acts Lincoln
did not report to Congress till nearly a year later, and by
that time they had long since become history.

The secession crisis, however, was only the first, although
the most urgent, of the crises with which Lincoln was called
upon to deal. On August 4, 1862, confronted with an imminent breakdown of voluntary recruiting, the President

[14] On this and the paragraphs immediately following see my *President,
Office and Powers* (2nd edition, New York University, 1941), pp. 155–66
and notes; and Carl B. Swisher, *American Constitutional Development*
(Boston, 1943), Chap. xiv.

instituted a militia draft. On September 24, in order to implement this measure and at the same time strike at the disloyalty that was rampant in certain of the northern States, he proclaimed a nation-wide suspension of the habeas corpus privilege as to all persons "guilty of any disloyal practice" and pronounced such persons to be subject to trial and punishment by courts martial and military commissions. And meantime he had issued the first draft of his Emancipation Proclamation, in which he declared that on the following January 1 "all persons held as slaves within any State or designated part of a State, the people whereof shall then be in rebellion against the United States, shall be then, henceforth and forever free," and pledged "the Executive Government of the United States, including the military and naval authority thereof," to recognize and maintain the freedom thus conferred.

What significance should be attributed to these extraordinary acts of Lincoln, undertaken in an era of *civil* war, as precedents for Presidential action in relation to a national *foreign* war? The question can be answered more precisely if we group the measures in question in four categories. The first comprises those of which the domestic enemy was the immediate target, the blockade of the Southern ports and the Emancipation Proclamation being the outstanding instances. While abounding in dramatic values, this category has no significance for our inquiry. Although the Court held in the Prize cases in 1863 that the President was entitled to treat the blockaded States as enemy territory and their inhabitants as "enemies" of the United States, and thereby put them out of their constitutional rights, the holding adds nothing to the President's conceded powers as Commander-in-Chief against a foreign foe. It should be noted, too, in passing that the Court took pains to accompany its ruling with the dictum that "under the Constitution, Congress alone has power to declare a national or foreign war."

The second category consists of measures which treated parts of the North itself as being in some sort a seat of war, the trial of civilians by military commissions affording the principal illustration. This category comes down to us seriously discredited by the decision in 1866 in the famous Milligan case. Yet even if we adopt the far more realistic opinion of the minority justices in that case, we still find that the only power it attributes to the President to supersede the ordinary courts by military procedures is in direct connection with his power in "command of the forces and the conduct of campaigns." Any broader power of this nature, it is clearly stated, must come from Congress. And both wings of the Court were in agreement that the military commission which had tried Milligan was contrary to the Act of Congress of March 3, 1863 governing such cases.

This leaves only the third and fourth categories as comprising significant precedents for total war, those acts which were designed by the President to meet a temporary emergency until Congress had time to act, the enlargement of the Army and Navy in 1861 and the militia draft of 1862 being the principal examples; and those acts which were of like character except for the fact that the President never laid them before Congress for its sanction inasmuch as they had had their full intended effect before Congress could be consulted, the closing of the Post Office to treasonable correspondence and the paying out of two millions of unappropriated funds from the Treasury being illustrations. These two categories, taken together, *assert for the President, for the first time in our history, an initiative of indefinite scope in meeting the domestic aspects of a war emergency*. They represent a reversion to primitive conceptions of executive power, which moreover were not left to inarticulate inference at the time. On this point counsel's summary of the government's argument in the Prize cases may probably be taken at face value. The argument rested, said counsel,

> upon a figure of speech which is repugnant to the genius of republican institutions, and, above all, to our written Constitution. It makes the President, in some sort, the impersonation of the country, and invokes for him the power and right to use all the forces he can command to *"save the life of the nation."* The principle of self-defense is asserted, and all power is claimed for the President. This is to assert that the Constitution contemplated and tacitly provided that the President should be dictator, and all constitutional government be at an end whenever he should think that "the life of the nation" is in danger.

Such high-flying views did not, naturally, escape challenge at the time. In his notable *Trial of the Constitution,* published in 1862, Sidney George Fisher urged that by English law "executive power, even in its primary and essential attributes, is subjected to legislative power," and that this principle was incorporated and even expanded in the Constitution of the United States. And on the floor of the Senate Charles Sumner early sounded a similar note:

> There are Senators [said Sumner] who claim these vast War Powers for the President, and deny them to Congress. The President, it is said, as Commander-in-Chief, may seize, confiscate and liberate under the Rights of War, but Congress cannot direct these things to be done. Pray, Sir, where is the limitation upon Congress? Read the text of the Constitution, and you will find its powers vast as all the requirements of war. There is nothing that may be done anywhere under the Rights of War, which may not be done by Congress. I do not mean to question the powers of the President in his sphere, or of any military commander within his department; but I claim for Congress all that belongs to any Government in the exercise of the Rights of War. . . . The government of the United States appears most completely in

an Act of Congress. Therefore war is declared, armies are raised, rules concerning captures are made, and all articles of war regulating the conduct of war are established by Act of Congress. It is by Act of Congress that the War Powers are all put in motion. When once put in motion, the President must execute them. But he is only the instrument of Congress, under the Constitution.

Sumner was right, of course, in contending that the prosecution of the war required the full exertion of the powers of Congress as well as those of the President. He was right too, technically, in describing the President's powers as those simply of military command; so the constitutional law of the day described them even as late as the Milligan case. He was deliberately wrong-headed in ignoring the cogent fact that President Lincoln had laid hold upon vast emergency powers that were not describable in the usual terms of military command, the results of which, nevertheless, Congress had accepted, willy-nilly; and in these regards the Civil War was the prototype of World War II.

In another respect the pattern of the Civil War was widely different from that of World War II. Because the former was fought at the national threshold, the President as Commander-in-Chief devoted great attention till 1864 to the war front, which, as we have seen, he regarded as embracing regions where disloyalty was rampant. For this reason, as well as because of his temperamental indifference to problems of administration, Lincoln left the leaders of Congress to take counsel respecting needed legislation from the individual members of his Cabinet whose departments were most immediately concerned, and especially from Chase and Stanton. It was thus that the two completely unprecedented measures, the Legal Tender Act of 1862 and the Draft Act of 1863, came about. The war was fought, in short, by a kind of diarchy. Only in the Act of January 31, 1862, which empowered the President, whenever "in his judgment the public safety shall require it," to take over any or all telegraph and railroad lines in the United States, together with their equipment and personnel, do we encounter a measure prophetic of the legislative phase of World War I and World War II, and a precedent for the collaboration of the two departments under Presidential leadership that was such an outstanding feature of those two wars on the domestic front.

In short, while conventional constitutional law even as late as 1866 still described the President's power as Commander-in-Chief, in Hamilton's terms in the *Federalist,* as the power simply to direct the operation of the national forces, yet the facts of the Civil War had shown conclusively that in meeting the domestic problems that a great war inevitably throws up, an indefinite power must be attributed to the President to take emergency measures, even though Congress is thus confronted with irremediable *faits accomplis* and a permanent set given to policy touching matters of vital importance to the nation.

5

I now propose to project against this background a brief account of "the War before the War." A question of dating presents itself. When the period ended is clear enough, thanks to Japanese treachery; when it began is more disputable. Something might be said for dating the *terminus a quo* of this momentous era October 5, 1937, for that was the day when President Roosevelt made his famed "quarantine speech" in Chicago. But was that speech so seriously intended as today it seems to have been? At the time many people waved it aside as just another of F. D. R.'s characteristically clever evasions, calculated to make people forget the embarrassing discovery that a recently appointed member of the Supreme Court had once belonged to the Ku Klux Klan; and no doubt the time will come when somebody will write a book, or at least an article, to prove the paradox that we made war on the Axis and its doctrine of race superiority because Justice Black once wore a white sheet and assisted in burning fiery crosses in order to spread fear of the white, gentile, Protestant God among Negroes, Jews, and Catholics!

Another possible date might be September 8, 1939, when Mr. Roosevelt proclaimed "a limited emergency"; or May 27, 1941, when he proclaimed an "unlimited" one. But by either of these dates the proclaiming of emergencies had become such an everyday affair with Mr. Roosevelt as automatically to rule them out as necessarily possessing landmark value.[15] Besides, just what feature of "the War before the War" are we most interested in for a study of the impact of war on constitutional structure? It is, I believe, the pattern of collaboration between the President and Congress at this period; and the culminating product of this collaboration was the enactment of H.R. 1776 as the Lend-Lease Act of March 11, 1941.

The first, faint impulse toward our participation in World War II was given quite without the intention of anybody by the enactment of the Trade Agreements Act of 1934, since then several times renewed.[16] Supplemented by other devices, the measure eventually became an instrument, on the one hand, for throttling Axis trade interests in Latin America and, on the other hand, for making our own trade with Latin America service our growing preparation for war. And the United States Shipping Commission, which was brought into existence in 1936 as an agency to build up a merchant marine, played in time a compara-

[15] See the *New York Times* of March 17, 1939, for a compilation by Mr. Bruce Barton of some thirty-nine instances of the use of the term "emergency" or some equivalent term by Roosevelt as President.

[16] For the matter of this and the immediately following paragraphs I am indebted to William K. Leonhart's *Executive Government in the Americas* (Princeton University Ph.D. thesis in Politics, 1943).

ble role. Through the Ships Warrant Act of July 14, 1941, which put all craft not holding the commission's warrants at a serious disadvantage in the use of American port facilities and in the procurement of needed supplies, the commission became an agency whereby all shipping resorting to American waters was compelled to become carriers of strategic materials for American defense agencies. Nor was the story of the Civil Aeronautics Act of 1938 essentially different. Intended primarily to encourage the development of an air-transport system adapted to then existing and future needs of commerce and the postal service, the act speedily grew in the hands of the President into a powerful weapon for combating the widespread activities of Axis air lines in South America. Similarly, export control, which the Neutrality Acts of 1935 and 1937, and even the amended Act of 1939, envisaged as a weapon of neutrality, was transformed in the Act of November 17, 1941 into the precise opposite of this; and meantime the "moral suasion" of the Department of State and "legislation by executive exhortation," as it has been called, had smoothed the way for this astonishing metamorphosis. And certain unrepealed sections of the old Trading with the Enemy Act of 1917, pieced out by later legislation, became the basis of Presidential proclamations under which, by July 1941, fully seven billions of Axis controlled assets in the United States had been frozen, and more than eighteen hundred individuals and firms doing business in the other Americas, where they were frequently the centers of subversive movements, were "blacklisted" — that is to say, were relaxed to the tender mercies of the British blockade.

Meantime, by the Strategic Materials Act of June 7, 1939 and an accompanying appropriation of one hundred millions, the Secretaries of War and of the Navy were enabled, with the approval and co-operation of certain of their departmental brethren, to procure stock-piles of such materials; while by the Byrnes Barter Act of August 11, 1939, but later greatly extended, RFC was enabled to offer loans to persons and firms willing to aid this program, an authority which that body exercised in part, with the aid of the laws of Delaware and the District of Columbia, by creating corporations with small initial capital, but enjoying unlimited borrowing power and complete immunity from public auditing. And to supplement all this machinery of war preparation, "preclusive buying agreements" were, by authorization of the President, entered into with various Latin-American states by an exchange of notes, the first one being with Brazil under the date of May 14, 1941.

Even yet we are not in the precise train of events leading to Lend-Lease. For this the starting point was furnished by an executive order early in 1938 by which the Army was directed to turn back older weapons to private contractors, who would then be free to dispose of them abroad, while replacing them with newer weapons for the Army. Nearly two years later, on December 6, 1939, to be precise, a liaison committee was established under the Secretary of the Treasury "to coordinate foreign military purchases with our domestic program." Then, on June 15, 1940, came the enactment of Public Resolution 83, which was designed as a pillar, in Mr. Arthur Krock's words, "of the Good Neighbor Policy and a vital part of the structure of hemisphere defense against the Axis." [17] The resolution provided:

> that the President, in his discretion, could authorize the Secretary of War to manufacture "or otherwise procure" munitions and implements of war on behalf of any American republic. He was authorized to "sell or deliver" this armament, test and repair it, and communicate any related information to the beneficiary American republic.
> The resolution provided also that the President could authorize the Secretary of the Navy to build war vessels for such

[17] *New York Times*, January 22, 1943.

republics, and armament and equipment for them, in any government shipyard or arsenal; to manufacture anti-aircraft artillery and ammunition for the same purpose; and to test, repair and communicate details.

Mr. Krock continues:

There was more to the bill. But it contained the proviso that no transaction under it should result in expense to the United States or involve the extension of credits. The dollar was the medium of exchange. At that time the Latin-American nations were obliged to equip themselves for defense in the arsenals and shipyards of countries in the Eastern Hemisphere because United States law barred them from purchases of material here. Public Resolution No. 83 removed that condition in the interest of hemispheric solidarity.

At this moment occurred the fall of France, and a like fate for Great Britain seemed only a matter of weeks. The startled Administration turned again to the above-mentioned Executive Order of 1938, and through private concerns as intermediaries more than half a million Lee-Enfield rifles and large stocks of heavier guns, as well as of ammunition, soon found their way to the hard-pressed British.[18] Then on September 3 it was announced that the United States had entered into an agreement under which, in return for the lease of certain sites for naval bases in the British west Atlantic, our government had handed over to Britain fifty over-age destroyers that had been recently reconditioned and recommissioned. Although the transaction was directly violative of at least two statutes and represented an assertion by the President of a power which by the Constitution is specifically assigned to Congress, it was defended by Attorney General, now Justice, Jackson as resting on the power of the President as Commander-in-Chief to "dispose" the armed forces of the United States,

[18] Thomas A. Bailey: *A Diplomatic History of the American People, Supplementary Chapters* (New York, 1942), p. 769.

which was ingeniously, if not quite ingenuously, construed as the power to *"dispose of"* them! [19]

Nor did the President ask Congress to ratify this extraordinary act as Lincoln had done when he increased the Navy in 1861. But when Congress appropriated money to build the bases the sites for which had been thus acquired, it in effect did ratify the agreement, and even more directly when it enacted the Lend-Lease Act, which, indeed, was a kind of extension and generalization of the destroyer deal.

But the destroyer deal was, after all, a temporary makeshift. If Britain was to remain in the war she needed a good many more things than destroyers, and to her acquiring these in the United States there were two formidable legal obstacles. As a belligerent she must, under the recently enacted Neutrality Act, pay for them "on the barrel head"; while as a defaulting debtor from World War I she was unable to borrow the needed dollars for purchases in the American market. What was to be done? It was while searching for an answer to this question that Oscar Cox, Assistant to the General Counsel of the Treasury Department, came across an act passed by Congress in 1892 which, slightly amended, still stands today on the statute book. It reads:

> Authority is given to the Secretary of War, when in his discretion it will be for the public good, to lease, for a period not exceeding five years and revocable at any time, such property of the United States under his control as may not for the time be required for public use and for the leasing of which there is no authority under existing law.[20]

[19] Bailey, op. cit., pp. 769–72 and citations; my communication to the *New York Times*, October 13, 1940; U. S. Code, tit. 34, §§ 492, 493a, 546e; tit. 18, § 33.

[20] U. S. Code, tit. 40, § 303. I am indebted to the courtesy of Mr. Cox for this reference. The Neutrality Act of November 4, 1939 is comprised in U. S. Code, tit. 22, §§ 441–57; the Johnson Debt Default Act of April 13, 1934 is to be found ibid., tit. 31, § 804a. Probably the property which the

Here at last is the *distinctive technique* of the Lend-Lease Act, the one that gives it its name, and the one that has been employed in its administration.

For the final steps in Lend-Lease's evolution we return to Mr. Krock's column:

> It was on a Friday morning, early in 1941, that the order came to draft the lend-lease bill. Secretary Morgenthau summoned to his office the youthful general counsel of the Treasury, Edward H. Foley, Jr., and told him what the President wanted. He also referred Mr. Foley to the Good Neighbor bill. Mr. Foley called in two of his assistants, also young lawyers: Oscar Cox, who is now Assistant Solicitor General, and Bernard Bernstein. . . .
>
> The three men worked all night and for a day and a night thereafter, drawing up lend-lease as an amendment to the earlier bill. On the instructions of the President they submitted it to Secretaries Hull, Stimson and Knox as well as to their own chief. All approved and initialed it. But Mr. Stimson suggested that the bill be drawn as a new measure, and not as an amendment, which was done. The President then initialed the draft, and in that form it was introduced and passed by Congress with very little change except to put a terminal date on the project and require frequent reports to Congress of lend-lease activities.
>
> Mr. Foley and his young collaborators put in the broadest language they could think of. But, though some of the sweeping phrases disturbed and continue to disturb friends of the idea, most of these survived the legislative process.

They surely did "put in the broadest language" — the broadest available from the dictionary. The Lend-Lease Act empowered the President for something over two years — it was later twice extended — whenever he "deems it in the interest of national defense," to authorize "the Secretary of War, the Secretary of the Navy, or the head of any other department or agency of the Government" to manu-

---

makers of the Act of 1892 had in mind was, for the most part, abandoned Army posts.

facture in the government arsenals, factories, and shipyards, or "otherwise procure" to the extent which available
funds made possible, "defense articles" — meaning thereby anything from butter to battleships — and "sell, transfer title to, exchange, lease, lend, or otherwise dispose of"
the same to the "government of any country [that is,
whether in exile or otherwise] whose defense the President
deems vital to the defense of the United States," and on any
terms that he "deems satisfactory." In brief, the act delegated to the President the power to fight wars by deputy; to
all intents and purposes, it was a qualified declaration of
war.[21]

6

The succeeding steps into actual, "shooting" war were as
follows: [22]

> March 30, 1941, the Government seized sixty-five Axis-
> controlled ships in American ports.
> April 9, the State Department entered into an executive
> agreement with the Danish Minister giving the United States
> the right to occupy Greenland during the emergency for de-
> fensive purposes. Protests by the Nazi-controlled regime at
> Copenhagen went unheeded.
> April 10, the President proclaimed the Red Sea no longer
> "a combat area," thereby making it permissible under the
> Neutrality Act of 1939 for American ships to carry supplies
> to the British forces in that region.
> May 15, the President appealed to the French people not
> to support the Vichy government, which, it charged, was col-
> laborating with the Nazis.
> May 21, the American steamer *Robin Moor* was torpedoed
> and shelled in the South Atlantic.
> May 22, the President gave Admiral Stark, Chief of Naval
> Operations, "an overall limit of thirty days to prepare for an

---

[21] U. S. Code (1940), Supp. IV, tit. 22, §§ 411–13.

[22] Most of the following items are culled from Bailey, op. cit., note 18
above, pp. 777–89.

expedition to sail for and take the Azores," [23] a project which was not, however, carried out.

May 27, the President, after declaring over the radio that the current developments of the war menaced the security of the Western Hemisphere, proclaimed an "unlimited emergency," and ordered American naval craft to "sink on sight" any foreign submarine discovered in our "defensive waters."

June 14, the President froze all previously unfrozen assets of Germany, Italy, and Axis-controlled countries.

June 20, the President sent a message to Congress denouncing the sinking of the *Robin Moor* as "piracy." The German chargé at Washington refused to transmit the message to Berlin.

July 7, the President announced to Congress that he had secured an agreement with the Icelandic government whereby the United States would take over from Great Britain the defense of that island during the emergency.

August 14, F. D. R. and Churchill announced that they had met at sea, "discussed lend-lease and other problems of common defense," and agreed upon a postwar "peace program," termed the Atlantic Charter. Thus, without consulting either the Senate or Congress, the President virtually committed the United States to a postwar alliance with Great Britain.

Meantime, though just when is not clear, the President had issued orders to the Navy to convoy supplies being sent to Great Britain under Lend-Lease as far as Iceland, a fact that he divulged in a message to Congress July 7; and four days later Secretary Knox confided to a Senate committee that "American warships were dropping depth charges in self-defense against Axis submarines."

September 4, Washington reported that a German submarine had fired two torpedoes in Icelandic waters at the United States destroyer *Greer,* but without effect. More than a month later the Navy Department revealed that the *Greer* had been trailing the U-boat for three and a half hours and broadcasting the latter's position when the submarine turned and attacked.

September 11, the President announced over the air that

[23] Admiral Stark's testimony before the Congressional Pearl Harbor Investigating Committee, *New York Times,* January 1, 1946.

"henceforth American patrols would defend the freedom of the seas by striking first at all Axis raiders ('rattlesnakes of the Atlantic') operating within American defensive areas." Isolationists in Congress charged the President with usurping Congress's power to declare war.

October 8, shooting orders were issued to United States warships in the Atlantic to destroy any German or Italian sea or air forces encountered. Indeed, at times American vessels operated under British command.[24]

October 17, it was announced that the American destroyer *Kearney* had been torpedoed off Iceland in what was later revealed to have been "a pitched battle" with German undersea craft.

October 27, "Navy Day," the President proclaimed that "the shooting has started."

October 30, the American destroyer *Reuben James,* engaged in convoying off Iceland, was torpedoed and sunk with the loss of about one hundred officers and men.

November 6, the President, finding the defense of Russia essential to that of the United States, pledged that country Lend-Lease aid to the amount of one billion dollars.

November 13, the House of Representatives, following the example set by the Senate six days earlier, voted 212 to 194 to repeal all restrictive provisions of the Neutrality Act of 1939.

The constitutional issue that emerges from this record centers chiefly on the matter of convoying. The Lend-Lease Act contained the provision that "nothing in . . . this title shall be construed to authorize or permit the authorization of convoying vessels by naval vessels of the United States." This phraseology betrays Congress's own uncertainty regarding its powers in the premises.[25] But the

[24] Admiral Stark's testimony, ibid., January 4, 1946.

[25] In enacting the Selective Service Act of September 16, 1940, Congress had betrayed no similar doubts as to its power to forbid outright the employment of "persons inducted into the land forces of the United States under this Act . . . beyond the limits of the Western Hemisphere except in the Territories and possessions of the United States, including the Philippine Islands." U. S. Code, tit. 50, § 303 (e) . By the Act of December 13,

President was uncertain too, as was shown by his repeated evasion of the issue when he was pressed to give an opinion; and his acts were not less evasive, as the Pearl Harbor investigation has amply shown. Convoying, first entered upon furtively, was by one device or another pushed gradually farther and farther across the Atlantic, and in the end a "shooting war" was precipitated without Congress having been consulted.

And what course was the Administration pursuing meantime with regard to Japan? As early as October 1940 the President was considering the throwing out of two sea patrol lines to halt all commerce from the Americas with Japan in case the latter took "drastic" action against Britain's reopening of the Burma Road, and was warned by Admiral Richardson that such a course would be an "act of war" likely to result in the loss of "many" American ships.[26] The following spring, staff conferences were held in Washington and Singapore which formulated plans for joint action by American, British, and Dutch forces in the Far East, and these agreements were approved by Secretaries Stimson and Knox. Then on November 28, 1941 the President and his "War Cabinet," composed of Secretaries Hull, Stimson, and Knox and Admiral Stark and General Marshall, came to the decision that the United States *must* fight if the Japanese attacked British Malaya, on account of the threat of such a move to the Philippines and other vital American interests. They also discussed the question: "How we should maneuver them [the Japanese] into the position of firing the first shot without allowing too much danger to ourselves"; and while the possibility of the Presi-

1941, this provision was suspended for the duration plus six months. U. S. Code, tit. 50 (War, App.) , § 731. Presidents have always exercised greater freedom in ordering the more mobile naval forces about than they have ventured to claim in relation to the Army.

26 See testimony of the Admiral in the *New York Times,* November 21, 1945 (William S. White's Washington dispatch) .

dent's sending Congress a message on the situation was broached,[27] the Administration in fact, as Senators Ferguson and Brewster point out in their minority opinion on the Pearl Harbor Investigation, "pursued from November 25th to December 7th tactics of waiting for the firing of the first shot by the Japanese."

To summarize briefly "the War before the War": The period falls into two parts. As early as 1938 the "good neighbor" policy, due to the growing menace of the European situation, was converted into the policy of hemispheric defense, and that in turn, on the fall of France, became the policy of making the United States "the arsenal of democracy." Throughout, the outstanding, the dominating fact is Presidential initiative, the constitutional synonym for which had been found by "Pacificus" one hundred and fifty years earlier in the opening clause of Article II. But there is Presidential initiative *and* Presidential initiative — that type which, recognizing that Congress has powers — great powers — in the premises, seeks to win its collaboration; and that type which, invoking the "Commander-in-Chief" clause or some even vaguer theory of "executive power," proceeds to stake out Congress's course by a series of *faits accomplis*. Prior to the enactment of Lend-Lease, Mr. Roosevelt generally employed the first type — the fifty-destroyer deal marking a conspicuous exception. After the enactment of Lend-Lease he preferred the second type, a course that must in the end have produced a serious constitutional crisis had not the Japanese obligingly come to the rescue.

Recording in his "Notes" for December 7, 1941 his reaction to the stupendous events of that day, Secretary of War Stimson wrote: "When the news first came that Japan

[27] Secretary Stimson's testimony and accompanying documents, ibid., March 22, 1946.

had attacked us, my first feeling was of relief that the inde-
cision was over and that a crisis had come in a way which
would unite all our people. This continued to be my dominant feeling in spite of the news of catastrophes which
quickly developed." [28] I have little doubt that this feeling
pervaded Administration circles generally.[29]

[28] The passage above quoted continues as follows: "For I feel that this
country united has practically nothing to fear; while the apathy and divi-
sions stirred up by unpatriotic men have been hitherto very discouraging."
This rather inconsiderately overlooks the real service of the "non-interven-
tionists" in having kept us out of war until Germany had attacked Russia.
We might have found ourselves in a pretty pickle had the "intervention-
ists" had it all their way.

[29] Representative O'Keefe says very aptly in his supplemental opinion
that "the concept of an 'incident' as a factor which would unify public
opinion behind an all-out war effort either in the Atlantic or Pacific had
influenced the thinking of officials in Washington for a long time. Many
plans which might have produced an incident were from time to time discussed and considered" — and it may be added, so far as the Atlantic was
concerned, were put into operation. See the *New York Times,* July 21, 1946.

II

The Impact of Total War

on the Powers and Structure of
the National Government

In the nearly one hundred and sixty years since the framing of the Constitution speculation regarding the nature and source of the war power has come full circle. In *Federalist* 23 Hamilton envisages the power of "common defense" as comprising a mosaic of particular delegated powers: "the authorities . . . to raise armies, to build and equip fleets; to prescribe rules for the government of both; to direct their operations; to provide for their support." He thereupon remarks that since "the circumstances which endanger the safety of the nation are infinite," so must the power to which the care of the nation's safety is committed "be coextensive with all the possible combinations of such circumstances." The assumption that any aggregate of specific powers can fulfill this requirement manifestly takes something for granted. As will be seen in a moment, accepted doctrine today avoids this difficulty.[1]

---

[1] The power provisions of the Constitution which contribute most directly to the war power are the following:

"The Congress shall have power to lay and collect taxes, duties, imposts and excises, to . . . provide for the common defense and general welfare of the United States" (Article I, Sec. 8, cl. 1) ;

"To borrow money on the credit of the United States; . . . To declare war . . ." (cl. 2) ;

"To raise and support armies, but no appropriation of money to that use shall be for a longer term than two years" (cl. 12) ;

"To provide and maintain a navy" (cl. 13) ;

Total War and the Constitution

The Constitution was still in its early infancy when counsel in the old case of *Penhallow* v. *Doane* [2] thought it pertinent to urge on the Court the view that the war power of the United States arises not from the Constitution, but from the sovereignty of the American people under the law of nations. Only two of the justices deemed it incumbent on them to notice the argument, one to accept it, the other to reject it. Sixty-nine years later, Lincoln, in his famous Message of July 4, 1861, accompanied his argument that the Union is older than the States with the repeated invocation of "the war power" as a single, unified power. Shortly following World War I the Court, speaking by Chief Justice White, declared "the complete and undivided character of the war power" to be "indisputable"; [3] and in his opinion for the Court in the Minnesota Moratorium case in 1934, Chief Justice Hughes voiced similar doctrine: "The war *power* of the Federal Government . . .

"To make rules for the government and regulation of the land and naval forces" (cl. 14) ;

"To provide for calling forth the militia to execute the laws of the Union, suppress insurrections and repel invasions " (cl. 15) ;

"To provide for organizing, arming, and disciplining the militia, and for governing such part of them as may be employed in the service of the United States, reserving to the States respectively the appointment of the officers, and the authority of training the militia according to the discipline prescribed by Congress" (cl. 16) ;

". . . To make all laws which shall be necessary and proper for carrying into execution the foregoing powers, and all other powers vested by this Constitution in the government of the United States, or in any department or officer thereof." (cl. 18) ;

". . . The executive power shall be vested in a President of the United States of America" (Article II, Sec. 1, cl. 1) . . . .

"The President shall be commander in chief of the army and navy of the United States, and of the militia of the several States, when called into the actual service of the United States . . ." (Sec. 2, cl. 1) .

It should be noted that the operation of most of these powers is not confined to time of war.

[2] 3 Dall. 54 (1795) .

[3] *Northern Pacific Ry. Co.* v. *No. Dak.*, 250 U. S. 135, 149 (1919) .

is a *power* to wage war successfully, and thus . . . permits the harnessing of the entire energies of the people in a supreme cooperative effort to preserve the Nation." [4]

It remained, however, for Justice Sutherland in his opinion for the Court in the Curtiss-Wright case in 1936 to supply the needed logical basis for the presumed unity and completeness of the war power by reverting to counsel's argument of 141 years earlier:

> A political society [reads the passage referred to] cannot endure without a supreme will somewhere. Sovereignty is never held in suspense. When, therefore, the external sovereignty of Great Britain in respect of the colonies ceased, it immediately passed to the Union.
>
> It results that the investment of the Federal government with the powers of external sovereignty did not depend upon the affirmative grants of the Constitution. The powers to declare and wage war, to conclude peace, to make treaties, to maintain diplomatic relations with other sovereignties, if they had never been mentioned in the Constitution, would have vested in the Federal government as necessary concomitants of nationality. [5]

But what difference, it may be asked, does it make whether the war power is a single "inherent" power or a complexus of delegated powers? This question has been partially answered already, at least in implication. It makes just this difference: under the delegated-powers theory silence on the part of the Constitution amounts to a *denial* of power, while under the inherent-power theory it amounts to an *affirmance* of power. The inherent-power theory thus logically guarantees the *constitutional adequacy of the war power by equating it with the full actual power of the nation in waging war*. It makes the full actual power of the nation constitutionally available.

This statement is subject, nevertheless, to an important

---

[4] 290 U. S. 398, 426 (1934) (italics added).
[5] 299 U. S. 304, 317–18.

qualification, except for which, indeed, these lectures might very well end at this point. *The inherent-power theory does not repeal specific provisions of the Constitution,* thus leaving a formless power. It obliterates neither those restraints on governmental action which result from the structure and constitutionally prescribed procedures of the National Government, nor yet those which result from the safeguards that the Constitution throws about private rights. In this lecture I shall deal chiefly with the effect of total war on the former kind of restraints, and in the lecture immediately following with its effect on the latter kind. The separation is, of course, merely for the sake of convenience, and when convenience dictates — as once or twice it does — will be abandoned. In reality constitutional liberty and the constitutional structure are mutually involved at every turn.

2

The "diplomatic front" was blown to bits at Pearl Harbor, but the "home front" burgeoned and flourished mightily. We turn now to the significant constitutional problems that arose on that front both in "the War before the War" and afterward. Not a few of these had been anticipated on the same front in World War I, and in the solutions which it brought to these World War I becomes to a remarkable extent a rehearsal for World War II.

Foremost of such problems was that of *adapting legislative power to the needs of total war.* Congress was suddenly called upon in 1917 to extend its power to a vast new range of complex subject-matter that had hitherto existed entirely outside the National Government's orbit, and at the same time to give its legislation affecting that subject-matter a form which would render it easily responsive to the ever changing requirements of a naturally fluid war situation. The solution of the problem was accomplished by the device that we saw exemplified in the Lend-Lease Act, the delegation of vast discretionary powers to the President to deal with a broadly defined subject-matter in furtherance of objectives equally broad. The Lever Food and Fuel Control Act, the impact of which on the normal rights of ownership will be pointed out later, vested the great powers that it brought into operation for the first time in our national history directly in the President, by him to be delegated to others; and numerous other measures conformed to the same pattern. The Selective Service Act vested in the President authority to raise an army by conscription; the Espionage Act vested authority to declare certain exports unlawful; the Priority Shipment Act authority to determine priority in car service; the Trading with the Enemy Act authority to license trade with the enemy and its allies, and to censor all communications by mail, cable, radio, or otherwise with foreign countries. Still other statutes clothed the President with power to regulate the foreign-language press of the country, to regulate the conduct of enemy aliens resident in the country and its possessions, to take over and operate the rail and water transportation systems of the country, to take over and operate the telegraph and telephone systems, and to redistribute functions among the executive agencies of the National Government.[6]

Ordinarily the President's first step in exercise of the powers thus conferred was to redelegate them in whole or in part to a designated agent or agents, while first and last their exercise involved the issuance in the name of the President, or with his implied sanction, of a vast mass of administrative regulations outbulking many hundreds of times the statutory provisions upon which they were ultimately grounded. In its governmental aspect the war was

[6] See my *President, Office and Powers* (New York University, 2nd ed., 1941), pp. 191–2.

fought by means of the administrative order, or, as we should say today, "the directive." Just whence this new terminology hails I have been unable to learn. The late Doctor Samuel Johnson would no doubt have dismissed it as "innovated without necessity," and so far as I can see he would have been quite right.[7]

In the Selective Service cases of 1918 [8] the constitutionality of this method of legislating was challenged in the name of the time-worn axiom that "the legislature may not delegate its powers." The Court failed to honor the contention with even a nod of recognition. Years later the same expedient was resorted to in combating the Great Depression, most conspicuously in that nine days' wonder, the National Industrial Recovery Act of 1933. This time the objectors to delegated legislation enjoyed a tumultuous field-day; one of the grounds on which the Court set the NIRA aside was that it delegated legislative power to the President improvidently and unconstitutionally.[9] Subsequent developments have nevertheless rendered the axiom hardly more than "a smoothly transmitted platitude" which is quite incapable of effective judicial implementation.[10] This is so today even in the field of domestic legislation; and on the diplomatic front it has apparently ceased to impose even a theoretical limit to the mergence by Congress of its powers with those of the President in the hands of the latter.[11]

Illustrative of the vast powers that were put at the disposal of President Roosevelt in World War II by Congres-

[7] One argument for "directives" as against "orders" is that the former is the longer word. Compare the current preference for "orientate" over "orient" and for "fissionable" over "fissile."

[8] 245 U. S. 366.

[9] *Schechter Bros. Corp.* v. *U. S.,* 295 U. S. 495 (1935).

[10] See *Hood and Sons* v. *U. S.,* 307 U. S. at p. 603 (1939); also *Opp Cotton Mills* v. *Administrator,* 312 U. S. 126 (1941).

[11] See case cited in note 5 above.

sional legislation are those which he exercised principally through the War Production Board (WPB). A section of the National Defense Act of June 3, 1916, still on the statute books, already authorized the President, "in time of war or when war is imminent,"

> to place an order with any individual, firm . . . or organized manufacturing industry for such product or material as may be required, and which is of the nature and kind usually produced or capable of being produced by such individual, firm . . . or organized manufacturing industry.

The act then continues: "compliance with all such orders for products or materials shall be obligatory . . ."; and any firm failing in compliance "shall be deemed guilty of a felony. . . ." [12] The Act of March 4, 1917 extended the above powers to the procurement of "such ships and war material as the necessities of the government, to be determined by the President, may require." Coincidently the President was empowered "to modify or cancel any existing contract" for the production or purchase of ships or war material; "to require the owner or occupier of any factory" for the production of ships or war material "to place at the disposal of the United States the whole or any part of the output of such factory"; "to requisition and take over for use or operation by the government any factory, or any part thereof . . ."; all which powers were to be exercised subject to the requirements of the Fifth Amendment respecting "just compensation." [13]

Then by Section 9 of the Selective Training and Service Act of September 16, 1940 the above powers were re-enacted and further reinforced by the penalty of plant-seizure; [14] and meantime by the Act of June 28, 1940 it was provided, in effect, that deliveries under all contracts and

[12] U. S. Code, tit. 50, § 80.

[13] Ibid., § 82.

[14] Ibid., tit. 50 — War, Appendix — § 309 (Supp. IV to 1940 ed.).

orders of the Army and Navy for war equipment should, "in the discretion of the President, take priority over all deliveries for private account or export." [15] The idea thus set going was soon greatly extended. By the Priorities Statute of May 31, 1941 it was enacted that the priority principle should reach, "in addition to deliveries under contracts of the Army or Navy, deliveries of material under":

> (A) contracts or orders for the Government of any country whose defense the President deems vital to the defense of the United States under the terms of the Act of March 11, 1941, entitled "An Act to promote the defense of the United States";
> (B) contracts or orders which the President shall deem necessary or appropriate to promote the defense of the United States; and
> (C) subcontracts or suborders which the President shall deem necessary or appropriate to the fulfillment of any contract or order as specified in this section.[16]

Furthermore, the President was authorized, "whenever . . . satisfied that the fulfillment of requirements for the defense of the United States will result in a shortage in the supply of any material for defense or for private account or for export," to "allocate such material in such manner or to such extent as he shall deem necessary or appropriate in the public interest and to promote the national defense." It should be noted that "this does not mean that supply must be inadequate to meet *war* demands alone. It means simply," as Mr. John Lord O'Brian, the able counsel of WPB explains, "that the total demand, including defense, civilian and export must exceed the supply," or the President may order the total available supply rationed. "This simple statute," Mr. O'Brian adds, "which is the basis of virtually all the present" (Mr. O'Brian was writing in

15 U. S. Code, tit 50 — War, Appendix — § 1152 (Supp. IV to 1940 ed.).
16 Ibid., § 633 (also § 1152).

42

1944) "far-reaching regulation of American industry, en- trusts to the Executive one of the most, if not the most sweeping grant of authority in our history." [17] And even this is not the whole story, for by the Second War Powers Act of March 27, 1942 authority to allocate "materials" was extended to "facilities," a power which, according to Mr. O'Brian, was widely exercised; and disobedience of WPB's directives, previously enjoinable, were made punishable as criminal offenses.[18] Yet of all the measures just passed in review, only this last one was enacted after Pearl Harbor.

Thanks, in part at least, to the intelligent and intensive campaign of education that WPB conducted among busi- ness men, its directives produced no important litigation requiring a judicial appraisal of the legislation recited above. With the Emergency Price Control Act of January 30, 1942 [19] it was otherwise. This act created the Office of Price Administration (OPA), headed by an Administrator to be appointed by the President with the advice and con- sent of the Senate, and conferred upon him authority to promulgate regulations fixing prices of commodities and rentals which "in his judgment will be duly fair and equi- table and will effectuate the purposes of this Act." These were stated to be: "to stabilize prices and to prevent specu- lative, unwarranted, and abnormal increases in prices and rents; to eliminate and prevent profiteering, hoarding," etc.; "to assure that defense appropriations are not dissi- pated by excessive prices; to protect persons with relatively fixed and limited incomes, consumers, wage earners from undue impairment of their standard of living," and so on.

[17] John Lord O'Brian and Manly Fleischmann: "The War Production Board, Administrative Policies and Procedures" (pamphlet, reprinted from the *George Washington Review* for December 1944), p. 11.

[18] See note 16. In §§ 633 and 1152 of tit. 50 — War, Appendix (Supp. IV), the statutory provisions distinguished in the text are all jumbled together.

[19] Ibid., §§ 901–46.

There were also further clauses purporting to be of a restrictive nature. Representatives of the industry were to be consulted "so far as practicable"; due consideration was to be given "to the prices prevailing between October 1 and October 15, 1941"; or if there were no such prices, then "to the prices that were prevailing during the nearest two-week period" which the Administrator found to be "generally representative." Certain possible abuses of power were banned, such as requiring restriction of the use of trade names, and so on and so forth.

In *Yakus* v. *the United States* [20] a defendant who had been convicted of violating orders of the Administrator contended that the act's declaration of purposes and the professed limitations on the Administration's powers were merely so much eyewash; but the Court thought otherwise. "The directions that the prices shall be fair and equitable," said the Chief Justice, "and that in addition they shall tend to promote the purposes of the Act . . . confers no greater reach for Administrative determination than the power to fix just and reasonable rates," so often sustained by the Court. The answer is yes, often sustained, but often disallowed too. The sober truth is that, while it has had a rather spotted history since it first emerged above the judicial horizon seventy years ago in *Munn* v. *Illinois*,[21] the term "reasonable rates" still possesses a substantial content that is often reducible to terms of dollars and cents.

The comparison urged by the Chief Justice was not a justified one. Justice Roberts dissented. "After showing," said he, "what needs no argument, that . . . [the] powers of Congress are very different from those exercised in peace, the Court then — without a sign that it realizes the great gap in the process — assumes that one of Congress's war powers is the power to transfer its legislative function to a

[20] 321 U. S. 414 (1944).
[21] 94 U. S. 113 (1876).

delegate. By the same reasoning it could close this court or take away the constitutional prerogatives of the President as 'war measures.' " And, he continues, while there are references in the opinion to the war emergency, "yet the reasoning of the authorities there cited seems to indicate that the delegation would be good in peace time in respect of peacetime administration." [22]

3

Unquestionably, the powers wielded by WPB in the theoretical capacity of adviser to the President, and by OPA in its own right theoretically, but actually subject to Presidential control through the Director of Economic Stabilization, exceed any previous pattern of delegated legislation touching private rights directly.

Yet even in the presence of war the Constitution does not altogether lose its capacity to recover equilibrium — or at least to seek to do so. At the same time that Congress has been broadening the scope of its delegations of power to the President, it has also been perfecting a technique to withdraw such delegations at will without the necessity of obtaining the President's consent, and this in face of the requirement of Article I, Section 7 of the Constitution that "every order, vote or resolution" to which the consent of both houses "is necessary" shall receive the President's approval before "they shall take effect." Thus, improving upon a precedent created by the Reorganization Act of April 3, 1939, the Lend-Lease Act, the First War Powers Act, the Emergency Price Control Act, the Stabilization Act, and the War Disputes Act, each and all contain provisions that make the powers they delegate subject to repeal at any time by "concurrent resolution" — that is to say, by a "vote or resolution" that under the rules of the houses is

[22] 321 U. S. at 459–60.

never laid before the President and hence is not exposed to his power of veto.

It is argued, to be sure, that this use of the "concurrent resolution" device is unconstitutional.[23] Yet it would seem to be no more so than its employment in any other connection save a vote of adjournment. The fact is, nevertheless, that concurrent resolutions have been employed for a great variety of purposes from the very beginning — for expressing the opinion of the two houses on this, that, or the other matter, for devising a common program of action, for creating joint committees, for directing the expenditure of funds appropriated to the use of the two houses, and even for proposing amendments to the Constitution — a practice that the Supreme Court has sanctioned from the beginning.[24] Then by the Reorganization Act of April 3, 1939 just referred to, by which broad powers were delegated to the President to regroup certain executive agencies and functions, it was provided that the President's orders to this end should be laid before the houses and be subject to their veto by "concurrent resolution" at any time within sixty days.

It is generally agreed that Congress, being free not to delegate power, is free to do so on certain stipulated conditions, as, for example, that the delegation shall terminate by a certain date or upon the occurrence of a specified event, the end of a war, for instance. Why, then, should not one condition be that the delegation shall continue only as long as the two houses are of opinion that it is working beneficially? Furthermore, if the national legislative authority is free to delegate powers to the President, then why not to the two houses, either jointly or singly? The Court has within recent years repeatedly approved delegations of

23 See Leonard D. White: "The Concurrent Resolution in Congress," 35 *American Political Science Review* 886 (1941).

24 See *Hollingsworth* v. *Va.*, 3 Dall. 378 (1798).

power to the Secretary of Agriculture to be exercised by him subject to the outcome of a referendum vote of producers from time to time.[25] Why may not the two houses of Congress be similarly authorized to hold a referendum now and then as to the desirability of the President's continuing to exercise certain legislatively delegated powers?

It is generally agreed, too, that the maxim that the legislature may not *delegate* its powers signifies at the very least that the legislature may not *abdicate* its powers. Yet how, in view of the scope that legislative delegations take nowadays, is the line between *delegation* and *abdication* to be maintained? Only, I suggest, by rendering the delegated powers recoverable without the consent of the delegate; and for this purpose the concurrent resolution seems to be an available mechanism, and the only one.

4

But by no means all Presidential directives were based immediately on Congressionally delegated powers, or on them at all. Many purported to spring directly from the President's constitutional powers as Chief Executive and Commander-in-Chief, or "Commander-in-Chief in wartime," although it was generally deemed good form — or perhaps the better part of valor — to cushion invocations of the President's constitutional prerogatives by references also to the First or Second War Powers Act, or simply to "the statutes" without more specific identification.

The most important segment of the home front thus regulated by what were in effect Presidential edicts was the field of labor relations. Just six months prior to Pearl Harbor, on June 7, 1941, Mr. Roosevelt, citing his proclamation thirteen days earlier of an "unlimited national emergency," issued an executive order seizing the North

[25] *Hood and Sons* v. *U. S.*, 307 U. S. 588 (1939); *Wickard* v. *Filburn*, 317 U. S. 111 (1942).

American Aviation plant at Inglewood, California, where, on account of a strike, production was at a standstill. Attorney General Jackson justified the seizure, the forerunner of many similar assertions of Presidential prerogatives, as growing out of the "duty constitutionally and inherently resting upon the President to exert his civil and military as well as his moral authority to keep the defense efforts of the United States a going concern," as well as "to obtain supplies for which Congress has appropriated money, and which it has directed the President to obtain." [26] On a like justification the Federal Shipbuilding and Dry Dock Co. at Kearney, New Jersey, was taken over and operated by the Navy from August 23, 1941, to January 5, 1942, and the plant of the Air Associates, Inc., at Bendix, New Jersey, placed under Army control from October 30, 1941 to December 27, 1941.[27] Then from the attack on Pearl Harbor to the enactment of the War Labor Disputes Act, June 25, 1943, Mr. Roosevelt ordered the taking over of the plants of four other concerns, one of them the Brewster Aeronautical Corp., the seizure of which was put on the ground of its "inefficient management"; another, the Toledo, Peoria and Western Railroad, which was destined to remain under the control of the Office of Defense Transportation (ODT) nearly three years and a half.[28]

Meantime, on January 12, 1942 Mr. Roosevelt had, by Executive Order 9017, created the National War Labor Board (WLB).[29] "Whereas," the order reads in part,

> by reason of the state of war declared to exist by certain resolutions of Congress . . . the national interest demands that

[26] New York Times, June 10, 1941.

[27] Report on the Work of the National Defense Mediation Board, March 19, 1941–January 12, 1942, Bureau of Labor Statistics Bulletin, No. 714 (1942), pp. 185–92, 194–9, 265–8.

[28] New York Times, March 22, 1942 and April 21, 1942; and Howard S. Kaltenborn: Government Adjustment of Labor Disputes (1943), pp. 129–30.

[29] 7 Fed. Reg. 237.

there shall be no interruption of any work which contributes to the effective prosecution of the War; and Whereas, as a result of a conference of labor and industry which has met at the call of the President on December 17th, 1941, it has been agreed that for the duration of the war there shall be no strikes or lock-outs, and that all labor disputes shall be settled by peaceful means, and that a National War Labor Board be established for a peaceful adjustment of such disputes. Now, therefore, by virtue of the authority vested in me by the Constitution and the statutes of the United States, it is hereby ordered: 1. There is hereby created in the Office for Emergency Management a National War Labor Board.

The order further provided that the board was to be composed of twelve special commissioners to be appointed by the President, of whom four should be representatives of the public, four of employees, and four of employers; and that it was to have "jurisdiction to settle all labor disputes likely to interrupt work which contributed to the effective prosecution of the war." Its jurisdiction was not to fall, however, until direct negotiations and the procedures of conciliation provided by the Department of Labor had proved fruitless and the dispute had been certified to it by the Secretary of Labor.

The effort of the Roosevelt Administration to govern labor relations without the aid of Congress was quite in line with Wilsonian policy in World War I, albeit with two important qualifications. While Mr. Wilson confined his appeals to his constitutional powers to wartime, Mr. Roosevelt, as we have seen, began basing action directly on the Constitution on the justification of "emergency" during "the War before the War." Again, whereas Mr. Wilson kept a fairly even hand as between labor and management, Mr. Roosevelt was constantly hampered by his ill-considered pledge at the beginning of World War II that labor should not be called upon "to sacrifice any of its gains." Taking advantage of this unwise commitment of the President and his own lighthearted view of the binding character of labor's no-strike pledge, the redoubtable head of the United Mine Workers succeeded in keeping the War Labor Board (WLB) and the Administration in hot water throughout the war, an example that spread its infection more or less widely in the ranks of labor generally. By the middle of 1943 the situation had become so unsatisfactory that Congress decided to intervene and enacted, over the President's veto, the War Labor Disputes Act of June 25, 1943, by which Presidential authority to commandeer struck plants was at last put on a statutory basis. But this was as far as Congress would go. When early in 1944 the President asked that body to pass a labor conscription act, it politely but firmly declined to share a responsibility which the President had up to that point sought to keep exclusively in his own hands.

5

The second important category of Presidential acts during and immediately preceding World War II which were of the nature of emergency legislation comprises orders establishing administrative agencies unknown to the statutes. Again the precedents established in World War I were followed with the qualification previously noted in the case of Presidential orders touching labor relations, that while President Wilson confined his acts of this character to the period of actual war, Mr. Roosevelt treated the preceding "emergency" as capable of fully activating his constitutional prerogatives.

Thus the War Industries Board, through which, headed by Mr. Baruch, industrial production was finally brought under a considerable measure of control and prices were to some extent regulated in the second year of World War I — which, in fact, once it was set up, quickly became the most important war agency in its operation upon civilian

life — was a purely Presidential creation. So too was the
Committee on Public Information, which, headed by Mr.
George Creel, performed the job that in the recent war was
divided between the Office of War Information (OWI),
headed by Mr. Elmer Davis, and the Office of Censorship
(OC), headed by Mr. Byron Price. Moreover, the medium
of Mr. Wilson's war labor policies was a War Labor Board
which, like Mr. Roosevelt's, was the product of Presidential
creative fiat pure and simple.[30]

In World War II and in "the War before the War"
which was its precursor, these patterns were reproduced on
a lavish scale — never, indeed, was a parcel of precedents
more generously blessed with progeny. In the latter part
of April 1942 I received from the Executive Office of the
President, in response to an inquiry, a list of forty-two
"executive agencies," of which thirty-five were of purely
Presidential creation. Eight of them, including the Combined Chiefs of Staff and the Combined Raw Materials
Board, were the joint creations of our own and certain other
governments, out of, so far as our government was concerned, existing official personnel; nor was their role intended to be more than advisory. The remaining twenty-
seven, however, were designed to operate and did operate,
during their existence, on the home front, and of most of
them the principal membership was non-official. Oldest of
all was the Office for Emergency Management (OEM),
which was created by an executive order dated May 25,
1940. I shall speak of it again in a moment. Others were
the Board of Economic Warfare (BEW), the National
Housing Agency (NHA), the National War Labor Board
(NWLB, or more shortly WLB), the Office of Censorship

[30] On the War Industries Board and its activities, see Bernard M. Baruch: *American Industry in War* (1941); "Universal Mobilization for War
Purposes," *Hearings before the Committee on Military Affairs*, 68th Cong.,
1st Sess. (March 11, 13, 20, 1924), pp. 1–144 *passim; New York Times*, April
7, 1918.

(OC), the Office of Civilian Defense (OCD), the Office of Defense Transportation (ODT), the Office of Facts and Figures (OFF), presently absorbed into the Office of War Information (OWI), the War Production Board (WPB), which superseded the earlier Office of Production Management (OPM), the War Manpower Commission (WMC), etc. Earlier there had been the Office of Price Administration and Civilian Supply (OPACS), but it had been replaced, as we have seen, under the Emergency Price Control Act of January 30, 1942, by OPA. Later OWI, mentioned above, was created by executive order, as was also the Office of Economic Stabilization (OES). The Office of War Mobilization (OWM), the last of the war agencies to appear, was established by the War Mobilization and Reconversion Act of October 3, 1944.[31]

What was the constitutional and legal status of these various "offices," "administrations," "authorities," "committees"? It is definitely stipulated by the Constitution that all civil offices except those of President and of Vice President (and perhaps those of ambassadors, public ministers, and justices of the Supreme Court) "shall be established by

31 U. S. Code, tit. 50 — War, Appendix — § 1651 (Supp. IV). For Emergency War Agencies that were functioning at any particular time, consult the *United States Government Manual* of the approximate date. The executive order creating an agency is cited by number. For a "Chronological List of Wartime Agencies" (including government corporations) and some account of their creation down to the close of 1942, see the excellent chapter on "War Powers and Their Administration" by Dean Arthur T. Vanderbilt in *1942 Annual Survey of American Law* (New York University School of Law, 1945), pp. 106–231. At the close of the war there were 29 agencies grouped under OEM, of which OCD, WMC, and OC were the first to fold up. At the same date there were 101 separate government corporations, engaged variously in production, transportation, power-generation, banking and lending, housing, insurance, merchandising, and other lines of business and enjoying the independence of autonomous republics, being subject to neither Congressional nor Presidential scrutiny, nor to audit by the General Accounting Office.

law," [32] and that all appointments to office shall be made by the President with the advice and consent of the Senate unless, in the case of "inferior officers," Congress shall provide otherwise. In the case of most of the war agencies Congress had not provided otherwise, or indeed provided at all.

In creating such an agency it was generally Mr. Roosevelt's practice to invoke his powers as President and Commander-in-Chief under the Constitution and the First War Powers Act. The latter reliance may be ruled out at once, both because several of the above listed agencies antedated its enactment and also because the act does not purport to authorize the President to create new offices but only to "make such redistribution of functions among executive agencies as he may deem necessary." [33] That the Administration was clearly aware of these constitutional difficulties is shown by its endeavor to evade them through the device of grouping its various creations under the roof-tree of the oldest of them, the Office of Emergency Management, which was in turn installed in the "Executive Office of the President." The process is one that might have been dragged out to even greater length without impairing the force of the axiom that zero plus zero is zero still.

The question of the legal status of the Presidential agencies was dealt with judicially but once. This was in the decision, in June 1944, of the United States Court of Appeals of the District of Columbia in a case styled *Employers*

[32] Article II, § 2.

[33] When Congress desired to authorize the President to *create* offices, it was able to do so in unmistakable terms, as in Sections 1 and 2 of the Lever Food and Fuel Control Act of August 10, 1917, whereby the President was authorized "to create and use any agency or agencies." Also in Section 2 (a) of the National Industrial Recovery Act of 1933, "to effectuate the policy of this title the President is hereby authorized to establish such agencies . . . as he may find necessary, to prescribe their authorities, duties, responsibilities, tenure," etc.

Group of Motor Freight Carriers v. *NWLB*,[34] which was a suit to annul and enjoin a "directive order" of WLB. The court refused the injunction on the ground that at the time when the directive was issued any action of the board was "informatory," "at most advisory." In support of this view the court quoted approvingly a statement by the chairman of the board itself:

> These orders are in reality mere declarations of the equities of each industrial dispute, as determined by a tripartite body in which industry, labor, and the public share equal responsibility; and the appeal of the Board is to the moral obligation of employers and workers to abide by the non-strike, no-lock-out agreement and . . . to carry out the directives of the tribunal created under that agreement by the Commander-in-Chief.

Nor, the court continued, had the later War Labor Disputes Act vested WLB's "orders" with any greater authority, with the result that they were still "judicially unenforceable and unreviewable."

Following this theory, then, WLB was not an "office" wielding power, but a purely advisory body, such as Presidents have frequently created in the past without the aid or consent of Congress. Yet *actually* the board generally proceeded independently of dictation from above and its "advice" was almost invariably "taken" — was not, in fact, even reviewed by the President. Indeed, this had to be the case if the board was to realize the purpose for which it was created, which was to provide a "tribunal" to effect settlements of labor disputes in which the three interests, the public, management, and labor, should have equal voice. And while WPB served a different purpose, it too exercised governing power which it would be purest fiction to characterize as "advisory." There were, to be sure, certain important differences between the two bodies. The powers that

34 No. 8680 (June 2, 1944).

WLB exercised prior to the War Labor Disputes Act [35] were supposed to be emanations from the President's power as "Commander-in-Chief in wartime," and were not supported by legal penalties or judicial process in any way, while the powers exercised by WPB were powers that the President had received from Congress, and were supported by legal penalties and equity process. Yet in both cases the advisory character of the agency was for the most part a sham and pretense, its *governing capacity* the substantial reality. In this respect neither board differed materially from OPA, whose head was appointed by the President with the advice and consent of the Senate and received his powers by direct delegation from Congress. Indeed, Congress itself both in its appropriation acts and in other legislation treated the Presidential agencies as in all respects "offices." Only that ancient spoilsman McKellar of Tennessee waged a protracted, albeit futile, war on them as "unconstitutional," and even he indicated that he could be appeased by subjecting appointments to them to Senate ratification. Just how this requirement would have rendered the agencies more constitutional, Senator McKellar did not profess to explain.

6

And this brings us to still another matter, closely related to those just dealt with, as to which the Rooseveltian war effort on the home front was once again indebted to Wilsonian precedents. I refer to what have been variously termed "administrative sanctions," "indirect sanctions," or simply "sanctions." The following episode involving the Remington Arms Company of Bridgeport, Connecticut, in the fall of 1918 will serve to illustrate the subject. The narrative is by a member of President Wilson's WLB:

[35] June 25, 1943; U. S. Code, tit. 50 — War Appendix — §§ 1501–11 (Supp. IV to ed. of 1940).

After a prolonged strike and the War Labor Board had rendered a decision against the strikers they refused to return to work. The President of the United States then wrote to the strikers upholding the authority of the Board, pointing out that an appeal from it should be made through the regular channels and not by strike. He closed with the statement that if the strikers did not return to work they would be barred from any war work in Bridgeport for a year, that the United States Employment Service would not obtain positions for them elsewhere, and that the draft boards would be instructed to reject any claim for exemptions based upon their alleged usefulness in war production. This ended the strike.[36]

Indeed, according to Mr. Baruch, chairman of the War Industries Board, that agency carried the indirect sanctions idea even farther at times. Violators of its orders, "when detected, were induced or coerced into forfeiting materials or making 'voluntary' cash payments to philanthropic organizations, to the United States Treasury, etc." That is to say, forfeitures and payments that were in essence legal penalties "were imposed and acquiesced in," although, as Mr. Baruch concedes, they were utterly devoid of legal authority. They were in fact nothing short of blackmail.[37] The two Presidential agencies which were most dependent in World War II upon indirect sanctions, inasmuch as, prior to the enactment of the War Labor Disputes Act, their directives were totally without support from legal penalties or judicial processes, were WLB and WMC. The case of the latter agency is particularly instructive.[38]

The business of this agency was to bring about and maintain the most effective mobilization of the man-power

36 *Hearings* cited in note 30 above, at p. 21.

37 O'Brian and Fleischmann, op. cit. in note 17 above, at p. 46.

38 In Executive Order 9370 of August 16, 1943 (8 *Fed. Reg.* 11463), we have direct evidence of the President's acceptance of the "indirect sanction" idea. The order was called forth by John L. Lewis's defiance of some of WLB's directives, and proved futile.

of the country that was available for war work after the armed services had taken their toll. Indeed, by Executive Order 9279, issued December 5, 1942, the President transferred the Selective Service System itself to WMC and thereby vested complete control of the man-power of the country not yet enrolled in the Armed Services in Chairman McNutt. By the same order, "Each Executive department and agency" was ordered so to "utilize" its facilities, services, personnel, and powers as the chairman of WMC, "after consultation with such department or agency, determines necessary to promote compliance with . . . the policies, directions and regulations" of WMC.[39]

Two months later — on February 3, 1943, to be precise — Mr. McNutt issued his famous "work or fight" order requiring all workers designated as "non-deferrable" — that is, as non-essential — to choose between induction into the armed services and transferring to essential jobs. The order carried, for those subject to draft, the penalty for disobedience on the face of it. At the same time, draft requirements were significantly lowered.[40]

A year and a half later WMC, now in control of eighty-five per cent of the working forces of the nation, decreed that henceforth all male workers in the United States were to be hired exclusively through USES (United States Employment Service), another Presidential agency that acted subject to WMC's directives. To effectuate this turn of policy the support of employers was of course necessary, and this was guaranteed in a variety of ways. As the *Labor Relations Reporter* explained it, for employers who do not string along with the program, "psychological pressure"

[39] 7 *Fed. Reg.* 10177. Prior to this, by Exec. Order 9247, September 17, 1942, the USES, certain defense functions of OE (Office of Education) and the employment functions of SSB (Social Security Board) and of the NYA (National Youth Administration) were transferred to WMC. 7 *Fed. Reg.* 7379.

[40] 8 *Fed. Reg.* 1996–7.

will be used at first, publicity to stir up community reaction, and then pressure from local management labor committees. In addition, they can have their power, lighting, and heat turned off and be deprived of shipping facilities and materials.

> The WMC stated [the *Reporter* continues], that government contracts might be withheld from employers found to be in willful and substantial noncompliance with the ceiling program. Since violators would have all their labor referrals and other manpower services cancelled, government procurement officers would be unable to renew or place contracts with such firms on the ground that they might be unable to manufacture the products specified for lack of available manpower.[41]

Sanctions so stringent, functioning mainly through employment ceilings and priority referrals, obviously approached the drastic character of a labor draft. If an employer had more workers than his ceiling, he was forced to give them up; if certain workers of a particular firm were needed elsewhere, the firm had to terminate their services and the workers had to transfer to the employment to which they were referred.

Two agencies there were whose orders were backed by legal sanctions, OPA and WPB. Yet OPA occasionally and WPB frequently resorted to "indirect sanctions." For, as Mr. O'Brian put it, "our concern is with the flow of materials, not the punishment of crime." He might have illustrated his remark by citing the case of three partners of a Chicago manufacturing plant who were permitted to take turns serving thirty days each in the county jail so as not to impede war production in their plant.[42] "Suspension orders," however, which were the shape that most of WPB's

41 *Labor Relations Reporter*, August 21, 1944.
42 *New York Times*, October 24, 1944.

indirect sanctions assumed, sent nobody to jail, although they might cripple the style of a recalcitrant producer temporarily. Moreover, suspension orders were much more expeditious than criminal prosecutions, or even than suits in equity. So when a Congressional committee proposed to forbid "any federal official the right to inflict or impose penalties, sanctions, or suspension orders of any kind" except as he was specifically authorized by statute to do, WPB protested vehemently. The proposal, said the board's spokesman, "would destroy our control completely. We might as well close up the Compliance Division" of WPB; and the protest prevailed for the most part.[43] First and last, WPB issued over seven hundred suspension orders, many times the number of prosecutions that the Department of Justice undertook at its behest.[44]

The problem of accommodating indirect sanctions to the Constitution arose out of the accepted doctrine that Congress alone may enact penalties and that no one may be subjected to a penalty that was not duly enacted by Congress prior to his alleged offense.[45] Not, however, till 1944 did

[43] While the proposal was not adopted, the federal district courts were given exclusive jurisdiction to enjoin suspension orders. 78th Cong., 2nd Sess. Public Law No. 509 (December 20, 1944); U. S. Code, tit. 50 — War Appendix — § 633, sec. 2 (a), (9). The enactment came too late in the war to have much effect.

[44] Thomas J. Graves: *The Enforcement of Priorities, Conservation and Limitation Orders of the War Production Board* (Princeton University Ph.D. thesis, 1946). Mr. Graves was a member of the Compliance Division of WPB. "More than three million PD-1A priority certificates were issued from January, 1941, through May 31, 1944; 5,353 orders, regulations and amendments were issued by the Office of Production Management and the War Production Board. There is no record available as to the individual directions and allocations issued. When it is recalled that all this gigantic spate of legal and executive activity finds its basis in three sentences of a statute, some notion can be gained of the scope and complexity of the undertaking from the standpoint of legal supervision and direction." O'Brian and Fleischmann, op. cit., note 17 above, at p. 28.

[45] *United States* v. *Eaton*, 144 U. S. 677, is the leading case. With characteristic legal acumen, general counsel of OPM perceived the problem

the Supreme Court finally become seized of the opportunity to reduce "sanctions" to some kind of constitutional regularity capable of differentiating the allowable type from straight-out administrative blackjacking. This was in the case of *Steuart and Bro., Inc.* v. *Bowles*,[46] in which a retail dealer in fuel oil in the District of Columbia was charged with having violated a rationing order of OPA by obtaining large quantities of oil from its supplier without surrendering ration coupons, by delivering many thousands of gallons of fuel oil without requiring ration coupons, and so on, and was prohibited by the agency from receiving oil for resale or transfer for the ensuing year. The offender

---

from the beginning, and the manner in which OPM, under his advice, sought to meet it is told by Mr. O'Brian in the following anecdote:

"In the fall of 1941, aluminum was the scarcest and the most urgently needed of all metals, being the limiting factor on the production of aircraft. Acquisition and use of it was strictly regulated. In this crucial situation, it was learned that a Chicago processor had obtained aluminum through false representations to the Board and had used it in the manufacture of parts for juke boxes. Of course the officials allocating aluminum wished to cut the concern off from future receipts or use of aluminum. In the conferences between the Aluminum Division, the Compliance Division and the Office of the General Counsel with respect to that case, there could have been observed the very birth pangs of a new chapter of administrative law.

"It was clear, of course, that it was a proper exercise of the allocation power to forbid the concern further transactions in aluminum. Certainly it cannot be argued that a statute which permits the President to allocate aluminum in such a manner as he finds 'necessary in the public interest and to promote the national defense' requires him to furnish the vitally scarce metal to one who had demonstrated that he will misuse it. On the other hand, there is unquestionably an incidental punitive element in the proposed action, and the lawyers were naturally concerned with thoughts of notice and hearing, due process of law, administrative absolutism and similar subjects. The decision that emerged was that the action proposed was proper but that before it could be taken the alleged violator must be notified of the charges against him and of the proposed action, and must be afforded an opportunity to be heard. The case proceeded along those lines and Order S-1, the first suspension order, was thereafter issued." O'Brian and Fleischmann, op. cit., pp. 48–9.

[46] 322 U. S. 598 (1944).

60

conceded the validity of the rationing order in support of
which the suspension order was issued, but challenged the
validity of the latter as imposing a penalty that Congress
had not enacted, and asked the District Court to enjoin it.
The court refused to do so and was sustained by the Supreme Court in its position. Said Justice Douglas, speaking
for the Court:

> Without rationing, the fuel tanks of a few would be full;
> the fuel tanks of many would be empty. Some localities
> would have plenty; communities less favorably situated
> would suffer. Allocation or rationing is designed to eliminate
> such inequalities and to treat all alike who are similarly situ-
> ated. But middlemen — wholesalers and retailers — bent on
> defying the rationing system could raise havoc with it. . . .
> These middlemen are the chief if not the only conduits be-
> tween the source of limited supplies and the consumers.
> From the viewpoint of a rationing system a middleman who
> distributes the product in violation and disregard of the pre-
> scribed quotas is an inefficient and wasteful conduit. . . .
> Certainly we could not say that the President would lack the
> power under this Act to take away from a wasteful factory
> and route to an efficient one a previous supply of material
> needed for the manufacture of articles of war. From the point
> of view of the factory owner from whom the materials were
> diverted the action would be harsh. . . . But in times of
> war the national *interest* cannot wait on individual claims
> to preference. . . . Yet if the President has the power to
> channel raw materials into the most efficient industrial units
> and thus save scarce materials from wastage it is difficult to
> see why the same principle is not applicable to the distribu-
> tion of fuel oil.

More briefly, indirect sanctions were constitutional when
the deprivations they wrought were a reasonably implied
amplification of the substantive power that they supported
and were directly conservative of the interests that this
power was created to protect and advance. Subjecting Mr.
McNutt's "work or fight" order to this test, it does not

come off well. To deprive an employer of his rights to certain priorities because he refused to pay a certain wage had no discernible tendency to forward the purposes for which the priorities system was instituted; and to send recalcitrant workers to the fighting front did not remedy the labor situation on the home front, but in the first instance actually impaired it by reducing the available stock of labor.

7

In the early case of *Little* v. *Barreme* [47] the Supreme Court, speaking by Chief Justice Marshall, ruled that the captain of a United States frigate who had seized a Danish vessel under orders issued by the President was liable for damages, the seizure having been made beyond the terms of an applicable act of Congress. This result was arrived at in face of the Chief Justice's undoubted belief that "the President of the United States, whose high duty it is to 'take care that laws be faithfully executed' and who is Commander-in-Chief of the armies and navies of the United States," might have, "without any special authority for the purpose, in the existing state of things, have empowered" the officer to do what he had done. The holding illustrates the then accepted doctrine that a constitutional act of Congress prevails over a conflicting but otherwise valid order of the President. In World War II this principle suffered some pretty hard usage at the hands of Mr. Roosevelt.

The outstanding illustration of Mr. Roosevelt's conception of the prerogative of the "Commander-in-Chief in wartime" vis-à-vis Congress is furnished by his peremptory demand upon Congress on September 7, 1942 that it repeal forthwith a certain provision of the Emergency Price Control Act of the previous January 30. I quote the salient pas-

[47] 2 Cr. 170 (1804).

sage from the President's remarkable address on that occasion:

> I ask the Congress to take this action by the first of October. Inaction on your part by that date will leave me with an inescapable responsibility to the people of this country to see to it that the war effort is no longer imperiled by threat of economic chaos.
>
> In the event that the Congress should fail to act, and act adequately, I shall accept the responsibility, and I will act.
>
> At the same time that fair prices are stabilized, wages can and will be stabilized also. This I will do.
>
> The President has the powers, under the Constitution and under Congressional acts, to take measures necessary to avert a disaster which would interfere with the winning of the war.
>
> I have given the most thoughtful consideration to meeting this issue without further reference to the Congress. I have determined, however, on this vital matter to consult with the Congress. . . .
>
> The American people can be sure that I will use my powers with a full sense of my responsibility to the Constitution and to my country. The American people can also be sure that I shall not hesitate to use every power vested in me to accomplish the defeat of our enemies in any part of the world where our own safety demands such defeat.
>
> When the war is won, the powers under which I act automatically revert to the people — to whom they belong.[48]

In a word, the President said to Congress: "Unless you repeal a certain statutory provision forthwith, I shall nevertheless treat it as repealed." On what grounds did Mr. Roosevelt rest his case for power of so transcendent a nature? Although he made a vague gesture toward "Congressional acts," it is obvious that his principal reliance was, and could only have been, on his "powers under the Constitution" — that is to say, his conception of these. Presidents have before this in a few instances announced that they did not consider themselves constitutionally obligated

[48] *New York Times,* September 8, 1942.

by something which Congress had enacted but which, as they contended, trenched on Presidential prerogatives. This, for example, was Johnson's position in 1867. But the position advanced by Mr. Roosevelt in the above quoted passage goes far beyond this, claiming as it does for the President the power and right to disregard a statutory provision which he did not venture to deny, and indeed could not possibly have denied, that Congress had complete constitutional authority to enact, and which, therefore, he was obligated by express words of the Constitution to "take care" should be "faithfully executed."

Nor did the first Roosevelt's celebrated "stewardship theory" of the Presidency furnish basis for the pretension advanced in the Message of September 7, since it stopped short with claiming for the President the right to do anything that he thought would be in the public interest, *provided he was not prohibited by the Constitution or an act of Congress from doing it*.[49] The Message of September 7 strikes this vital reservation out, at least so far as acts of Congress are concerned. The doctrine of the message answers, indeed, to John Locke's definition of "prerogative" "as the power to act according to discretion for the public good, without the prescription of the law and *sometimes even against it*" — a notion derived from Stuart practice, and one against which the framers unquestionably thought they had provided by the "faithfully executed" clause.[50]

The Message of September 7 can only be interpreted as a claim of power on the part of the President to suspend the Constitution in a situation deemed by him to make such a step necessary. The claim was not a totally unprecedented one, for Lincoln implied as much when in his Message of July 4, 1861 he asked, with reference to his suspension of the writ of habeas corpus: "Are all the laws *but one* to go

49 Theodore Roosevelt: *Autobiography* (1913), pp. 388–9.
50 *Second Treatise on Civil Government*, Chap. xiv.

unexecuted, and the Government itself go to pieces lest that one be violated?" But Mr. Roosevelt was proposing to set aside, not a particular clause of the Constitution, but its most fundamental characteristic, its division of power between Congress and President, and thereby gather into his own hands the combined power of both. He was suggesting, if not threatening, a virtually complete suspension of the Constitution. No doubt any candid person must admit that the circumstances of total war may render such a measure necessary, but surely Congress, if on hand at the time, ought to be associated in so grave a responsibility, the need for which would presumably be evident to it also.

And certainly Mr. Roosevelt did not improve his case when he said: "When the war is won, the powers under which I act automatically revert to the people — to whom they belong." The implication seemed to be that the President owed the transcendent powers he was claiming to some peculiar relationship between himself and the people — a doctrine with a strong family resemblance to the Leadership principle against which the war was supposedly being fought.

And while the Message of September 7, 1942 marked the high point in F. D. R.'s *explicit* claims for Presidential prerogative, certain other of his acts imply a close approximation to the doctrine of that message. The fifty-destroyer deal, especially when it is considered in the light of Attorney General Jackson's effort to justify it, is just such an approximation. But on the home front, too, episodes occurred that at least implied a claim to dispense with the statutes. One such episode was the President's order of October 27, 1942 to Economic Stabilization Director Byrnes to set a twenty-five-thousand-dollar limit to all salaries. In theory this directive was based on a provision of the Stabilization Act of October 2, 1942,[51] which authorized the Presi-

51 Chap. 578, 56 Stat. 765.

dent to reduce salaries or wages "to the extent that he finds necessary to correct gross inequities and to aid in the effective prosecution of the war." Certainly this language is broad enough standing by itself to justify almost any construction — an order, for instance, reducing salaries to one thousand dollars a year. But in fact the provision did not stand by itself, for the President was well aware that Congress, in the course of considering the measure, had rejected the precise proposal embodied in his directive; and in the Act of April 12, 1943, raising the public debt limit from one hundred and twenty-five billions to two hundred and ten billions, Congress incorporated a provision that explicitly rescinded the order. The President was sorely vexed, and in a public statement expressed his deep regret that the needs of the Treasury would not admit of his vetoing the bill. He also protested strongly against the practice of "attaching extraneous riders to any bill." [52] Yet if it be conceded that Congress itself knew better than the President what it meant when it enacted the statutory provision that Executive Order 9250 purported to interpret, this protest leaves one rather cold.

And F. D. R.'s acceptance early in the war of organized labor's demand that employers be required, as a condition of labor's not striking for the duration, to write a "maintenance of membership" clause in all their contracts of employment is off the same piece of cloth. In *National Labor*

[52] *New York Times*, April 12, 1943. The *Times* commented editorially: "The passage of the repealer should have removed the last possible doubt in the President's mind concerning the powers that Congress intended to confer upon him. His statement that he would have vetoed such a repealer standing by itself is nothing less, therefore, than a statement that he would have assumed this legislative power in defiance of the declared will of the majority of Congress. If anything were lacking to justify the action of Congress in attaching the repealer as a rider to a bill that the President had to sign, the President's statement has itself supplied the lack. So far as the constitutional issue is concerned, Mr. Roosevelt has placed himself in an untenable position."

Relations Board v. *Electric Vacuum Cleaner Co.*,[53] which
was decided practically contemporaneously with the appearance of the maintenance-of-membership issue, the Supreme Court held that such a clause, in the absence of a
closed-shop contract, was violative of the National Labor
Relations Act; and it was partly in reliance on this holding
that Montgomery Ward, after first yielding to the President's demands in the matter, in support of which Mr.
Roosevelt made the customary invocation of his powers
as "Commander-in-Chief in wartime," decided thirteen
months later to defy him, and thereby precipitated the
drama of April 26, 1944 in which Sewell Avery, president
of Ward's, Sergeant Jacob Lepak of Milwaukee, and Private
Cecil Dies of Nashville played the leading roles. In *Life's*
snapshots of the event Avery, in process of being gently but
firmly removed from his Chicago office, looks pretty grim,
yet not utterly unaware that he and Gray's "Village Hamp-
den" were brothers-at-arms.[54]

The original quarrel between the Administration and
Ward's was now displaced by the question of the validity
of the seizure of the Chicago plant. The question of the
scope of the President's power as "Commander-in-Chief in
wartime" still remained, however, and in more exagger-
ated form, while with it was combined a fresh question of
statutory interpretation. Required by his duty as family
lawyer of the Administration to defend the seizure, Attorney General Biddle, who allegedly had advised the President against the step, cited first a provision of the War
Labor Disputes Act which authorized the President to
seize any "plant, mine or facility equipped for war produc-

[53] 315 U. S. 685 (March 30, 1942). See also Attorney General Biddle's
opinion of December 29, 1942, that a maintenance-of-membership rule was
forbidden as to railway employees by the Railway Labor Act of May 20,
1926, as amended by the Act of June 21, 1934.

[54] See the narrative in the *New York Times* of April 27, 1944.

67

tion" whenever operation of the same was interrupted "by strike or other labor disturbance." But *was* Ward's Chicago plant "equipped for war production"? Quite understandably dubious on that point, Mr. Biddle went on to invoke also what he termed "an aggregate of powers" belonging to the President from the Constitution and certain unidentified statutes.

At this point an opportune diversion by the Administration enabled the Attorney General to revamp his argument still further. At seven p.m. central war time on May 9, the government suddenly withdrew from Ward's, not to return until the Presidential campaign was safely over. In support of the President's order of December 28 commanding the seizure of Ward plants at Chicago, Detroit, St. Paul, Denver, Portland, and other places,[55] Mr. Biddle, while not yet abandoning the argument he had erected on the War Disputes Act, brought forward a totally new and far less sweeping constitutional argument.[56] This was that the President as "Commander-in-Chief in wartime" had power "to requisition property for military purposes," a contention that the Attorney General backed up by citing the seizure by Union forces during the Civil War of three steamers on the Mississippi for the transportation of supplies for the Army. The alleged precedent, weak on the face of it, becomes even weaker when it is considered in the light of the language of the Supreme Court in passing on it. Citing the well-known opinion of Chief Justice Taney in *Mitchell* v. *Harmony*,[57] the Court particularly stressed the proposition there stated that to justify such a measure "the public danger must be immediate, imminent and impending,"

[55] Exec. Order 9508, 9 *Fed. Reg.* 15079.

[56] I am following the Brief for the United States in the Circuit Court of Appeals.

[57] 13 How. 115 (1852).

"the emergency in public service must be extreme and imperative." [58]

The final upshot of the Ward case was very disappointing. The government, after having its arguments snubbed or rejected outright by the United States District Court in Chicago, succeeded in getting the Court of Appeals there to rule that Ward's was "a plant engaged in war production," but failed entirely to obtain judicial countenance for its constitutional arguments.[59] Ward's then took an appeal to the Supreme Court, but the day before argument was to be had the Administration, repeating its exploit of the previous year, pulled its agents out of all of Ward's plants; whereupon the Court, accepting the Administration's contention that the case had become "moot," struck it from the docket.

Commenting on this ruling, a New York paper pertinently, if a bit heatedly, remarked:

Under this ruling, the only thing the bureaucrats need concern themselves about, apparently, is to end their imposi-

[58] *United States* v. *Russell*, 13 Wall. 623 (1872).

[59] *National War Labor Board* v. *Montgomery Ward and Co.*, 144 Fed. (2nd) 528; *United States* v. *Montgomery Ward and Co.*, 152 Fed. (2nd) 369 (C. C. A. 7th). The Circuit Court of Appeals rested its holding that Ward's was a "producing" concern on Section 203 (j) of the Fair Labor Standards Act of 1938, which reads: " 'Produced' means produced, manufactured, mined, *handled, or in any other manner worked on* in any State; and for the purposes of this chapter an employee shall be deemed to have been engaged in the production of goods if such employee was employed in producing, manufacturing, mining, *handling, transporting, or in any other manner working on such goods, or in any process or occupation necessary to the production thereof,* in any State." Applying this provision in *Western Union Teleg. Co.* v. *Lenroot*, the Supreme Court had ruled (January 8, 1945) that telegraphic messages are "goods" which Western Union "produces" in the sense of the above quoted section. 323 U. S. 490. To be sure, the statute involved in the Ward case was the War Labor Disputes Act, not the Fair Labor Standards Act; but no doubt the circuit judges felt that they ought to be just as free to perform linguistic somersaults as Congress is.

tions before the day when the citizen's appeal comes up for a ruling in the Supreme Court. Up to that day they could do as they liked with the citizen's property or his rights. They could confiscate his property without authority or impose illegal restrictions and regulations upon him for a period of weeks, months or years, but by merely returning the property or lifting the regulations at the opportune time they could prevent his demand for constitutional justice from ever being heard.[60]

But the blame for the fiasco was partially Ward's too. Instead of bringing its case solely in equity, Ward's should also have sued the government's agents in trespass. Then their withdrawal would not have automatically killed the case.[61]

8

As we saw early in this lecture, federalism as a system of counterpoise is no longer viable in the field of war-making or in the sphere of foreign relations at all. As a system of collaboration, on the other hand, it can be a very vital factor of the war effort on the home front, a fact that meets early expectations. For the belief that the National Government would frequently employ the State authorities in the carrying out of its powers was asserted both on the floor of the Philadelphia Convention and in the *Federalist,* and is testified to by much early legislation.[62] Later, nevertheless, this belief came to be undermined both with Congress and

[60] *Journal American,* issue of November 13, 1945.

[61] See e.g., *Bell* v. *Hood,* decided April 1, 1946. Ward's, if we are to believe its spokesman, was the victim at the time of the first seizure of a very extreme form of "indirect sanction." According to a telegram that the firm sent the President, "The United States Post Office, presumably acting on order from Washington, removed its seventy employees from the mail order house. For more than thirty years the Post Office had maintained this department for the purpose of handling parcel post shipments to Ward's customers." *Montgomery Ward's Statement to the Special Investigating Committee of the House of Representatives* (June 6, 1944) , p. 3.

[62] On the above paragraphs, see my *Court over Constitution* (Princeton, 1938) , pp. 133–47, with references.

the Court by the rising tide of States-rightism, and on the
very eve of the Civil War we find the Court proclaiming,
in terms that must have been highly gratifying to the se-
cessionist leaders, that Congress had no power to impose
any duty "on a State officer as such and compel its perform-
ance." To be sure, the Court indicated, the States might
still aid the National Government in the enforcement of
its laws, but that would be of their own free choice. Their
co-operation would not be of the kind that was suggested
to the small boy by teacher's statement that he must "cooperate." "I know," he commented brightly, "what 'cooperate' means — it means I've got to do it."

It is interesting to compare in this connection a judicial
dictum uttered in 1820 with a statement from Lincoln's
Attorney General in 1862. Discussing in *Houston* v. *Moore*
on the former occasion the provision that Congress had
made for summoning the State militias into the national
service, Justice Johnson remarked: "The doctrine must be
admitted that Congress might, if they had thought proper,
have authorized the issuing of the President's orders even
to the Governor." But when Lincoln turned to the governors for aid in recruiting the Army during the first two
years of the Civil War, he was told by Attorney General
Bates that any assistance by them must be ascribed solely
to "the impulse of a generous humanity and patriotism."
In the end the reliance failed, and resort had to be had to a
draft carried into effect by federal officials.[63]

In the Selective Service Act of 1917 the earlier idea recurs. As Miss Jane Perry Clark writes in her illuminating
volume *The Rise of a New Federalism:*

> The need for utilizing state officers to aid in the great task
> was realized and provided for in no uncertain terms. It was
> made mandatory for state officers to assist the federal govern-
> ment in the administration of the whole Selective Service

[63] 5 Wheat. 1, 40 (1820) ; *Official Records,* etc. Ser. III, Vol. II, 151.

Act. In actual practice, the President did not give his orders directly to state officials but issued them through the state governors. For instance, state adjutants general of the National Guard were designated as state draft executives. State officials were also found useful when there came a need for appeal agents to present the viewpoint of the federal government in the hearings of all those who sought discharge on account of dependents. There were in all 192,688 employees who functioned directly under state superiors, while the office of the federal Provost Marshal General had only 429 Federal employees throughout the states.[64]

The Selective Training and Service Act of 1940, to be sure, abandoned this pattern, being applied through local boards appointed by the President "from recommendations made by the respective governors or comparable executive officials" and operating under "rules and regulations prescribed by the President." Even so, the recent war effort witnessed an immense amount of voluntary co-operation at all levels of service on the part of the State and local governments.

According to Dean Vanderbilt, the outbreak of World War II found still lingering on State statute books from World War I laws covering more than fifty topics, ranging from Aliens, Armories, Disloyalty, Flags, Food, Fuel, to National Anthem, Nurses, Treason, Voting, War, Wills. And the only objection that legalistic casuistry had been able to conjure up against this type of legislation was that since war is the business of the National Government, for a State to collaborate in its waging was to stray beyond the periphery of State competence, an objection that the Court brushed aside in these words:

> The United States is composed of the States, the States are constituted of the citizens of the United States, who also are citizens of the States, and it is from these citizens that armies

[64] Op. cit. (Columbia University Press, 1938) , p. 91.

are raised and wars waged, and whether to victory and its benefits, or to defeat and its calamities, the States as well as the United States are intimately concerned. And whether to victory or defeat depends upon their morale, the spirit and determination that animates them. . . . Cold and technical reasoning in its minute consideration may indeed insist on a separation of the sovereignties and resistance in each to any cooperation from the other, but there is opposing demonstration in the fact that this country is one composed of many and must on occasions be animated as one and that the constituted and constituting sovereignties must have power of cooperation against the enemies of all.[65]

In brief, being all in the same boat, all were entitled, even if not required, to lend a laboring oar.

The participation of the States in World War II began before actual war broke. It was foreshadowed as early as August 1940, when a Federal-State Conference on Law Enforcement Problems of National Defense was summoned by the Governors' Conference, the Council of State Governments, the National Association of Attorneys-General, and the Interstate Commission on Crime, in co-operation with the Department of Justice. Under the supervision of the Conference, model State legislation was prepared on State councils, defense, sabotage-prevention, State home-guard mobilization, and other subjects. Early the following year, by good fortune, all but four of the State legislatures convened, and many of them proceeded to organize their respective governments for emergency along the lines that had been laid down by the Federal-State Conference. The State Defense Council Act was adopted in twenty-one States. In several States large emergency powers were delegated to the governors. By the New Jersey statute, for example, the governor was directed to render the United States any assistance in the existing crisis within the power of the State, and to that end to organize and employ any and all re-

[65] *Gilbert* v. *Minn.*, 254 U. S. 325 at 329 (1920).

sources of the State, whether of men, property, or instrumentalities.[66]

The New York State War Emergency Act of 1942, later several times amended, was more elaborate. It created a State War Council with power "to cooperate with agencies established by and pursuant to laws of the United States and of the several States to promote civilian protection and the war effort." More specifically, the council was empowered "to adopt and promulgate any rationing, freezing, price fixing or other order or regulation imposed by the authority of the Federal Government; and to adopt rules and issue orders with respect to the enforcement of any such rationing, freezing, price fixing or other order or regulation." At the same time orders of the council regarding black-outs, traffic, and certain other matters were vested with penal sanctions, a provision that was subsequently extended to the council's orders on all matters within its jurisdiction.[67]

Proceeding along these lines, the council in April 1943 adopted a resolution giving OPA rules and regulations the effect of State law and making violations thereof punishable in the State courts, action that was in due course sustained by a unanimous ruling of the Court of Appeals; and a year later the council's adoption of OPA'S regulations was extended to July 1945.[68] In all, says Dean Vanderbilt, about 600 acts relating to the war were passed by the States in 1941 and 1942.[69]

But the course of National-State co-operation, like that of true love, did not always run smooth. In fact, during the Presidential year of 1944 it often showed signs of becoming

[66] Vanderbilt, op. cit., in note 31 above, at pp. 203–4.

[67] See *New York State War Emergency Act and Other Emergency Laws,* 1941, 1942, 1943, 1944, and 1945 (compiled and published by New York State War Council, July 1, 1945), pp. 9–73 *passim.*

[68] *New York Times,* April 28 and December 30, 1943; and May 4, 1944.

[69] Vanderbilt, op. cit., p. 205.

badly worn in spots, owing in part perhaps to the fears professed by partisan critics of the Administration of the continuance of "federal domination" after the war should be over, and sometimes there were personal factors.

In no area of the entire country was local co-operation more invaluable to the home front than in New York City, but it was not always forthcoming in full measure. That would have been too much to expect of New York's ebullient Mayor, the eternally efflorescent "Little Flower." Fairly early in the war Mayor La Guardia withdrew police co-operation from OPA in the enforcement of its ban on pleasure driving; and the New York City agencies at no time attempted to enforce liquor price ceilings although the State War Emergency Act of course empowered them to do so.[70] But the really classic exhibition by the Mayor of his talent for posturing as the tribune of "his" people was called forth by Mr. Byrnes's "curfew request" of February 28, 1945. Mr. Byrnes asked that operators of clubs, restaurants, bars, movies, and so forth should, in the interest of conserving fuel, electricity, and man-power, close their establishments at midnight. After nearly three weeks of more or less spotty compliance in New York City, which was featured by arrests of patrons, the Mayor suddenly announced that the curfew would be "eased" to one a.m. Mr. Byrnes, backed by the President, protested vigorously.

> I recognize [said the Director of OWM] that the indirect sanctions, which are available to the Federal Government, do not lend themselves to the enforcement of such a request except in isolated instances of non-compliance. The available indirect sanctions cannot be effectively applied without the full cooperation of local authorities. The Government has no police force of its own available to discover local violations. It has no intention of building up such a force. It is

[70] *New York Times,* May 14, 1945.

obvious that this effort would in itself be a diversion from the war effort.[71]

In these words is indicated the chief value of State and local co-operation at the administrative level: thanks to the indefinite scope of their police powers, the State and local governments were able to supply the deficiencies of indirect sanctions when voluntary compliance failed. In the instance of the Byrnes curfew, however, the Mayor's headstrong course transferred the shoe to the other foot. Into the gap which his recalcitrance created WPB promptly stepped with threats to invoke man-power ceilings against noncompliant restaurateurs and all others in like case, to strip them of all but maintenance men, to cut off coal, gas, electricity, and other essentials, and so on. This stern attitude, backed by the activity of MP's and the Navy's shore patrols in seeing that service men were cleared out of places of amusement and refreshment by midnight, proved fairly effective.[72] Gradually the Little Flower's feud with OWM, from being front-page stuff, oozed out of the news altogether as Patton's forces began fanning out over Germany.

By way of summary: The constitutional aspects of our participation in World War II may be assessed for their relation to the preceding *constitutional law of war,* or as foreshadowing the succeeding *constitutional law of peace.* From the former point of view the difference between World War I and World War II is chiefly that which resulted from the vastly greater scope of the national war effort in World War II. It was undoubtedly in consequence of World War I that the Supreme Court in 1936 went out of its way to extend its approval to the conception of the war power as an inherent power, thereby formally dismissing federalism as a system of counterpoise, though not as a

[71] Ibid., *New York Times,* March 1, 6, 19, 20, 1945.
[72] Ibid., March 25, 1945.

system of collaboration, from the constitutional law of war. And meantime the Wilson Administration had under the pressure of war itself performed a kindred operation upon the doctrine that the legislature may not delegate its powers. The further indebtedness of F. D. R. to Woodrow Wilson for legal expedients useful on the home front in wartime I have shown in detail. Presidentially created war agencies performing the functions of regularly established offices; orders or "directives," having the technical status of advice to the President, but the actual effect of legal orders; "administrative sanctions" meant to do the work of duly enacted penalties — all these were weapons that Mr. Roosevelt found ready to hand in the arsenal of precedents left behind by his predecessor and that he applied on an unprecedented scale, not only without interference from Congress, but with its apparent approval. Yet despite its generally acquiescent attitude Congress did not altogether escape being flouted by the "Commander-in-Chief in wartime," and in the President's Message of September 7, 1942 is set the most exorbitant claim for Presidential power ever made by a President.

The predictive value of the home-front phase of World War II for constitutional law in the years to come is an altogether different matter, but one of the greatest importance. What was done in World War II, even when it was merely repetitive of what had been done in World War I, partly because it was repetitive, possesses a significance for the constitutional law of the future that could not possibly have been asserted of the precedents of World War I at the time. This is a matter I shall deal with in my final lecture.

III

The Impact of War on Constitutional Rights

Sir, in the authority given to Congress by the Constitution of the United States to declare war, all the powers incidental to war are, by necessary implication, conferred upon the government of the United States. Now, the powers incidental to war are derived, not from the internal municipal sources, but the laws and usages of nations. . . . There are, then, in the authority of Congress and in the Executive, two classes of powers altogether different in their nature and often incompatible with each other — war power and peace power. The peace power is limited by regulations and restricted by provisions in the Constitution itself. The war power is only limited by the usages of nations. This power is tremendous. It is strictly constitutional, but it breaks down every barrier so anxiously erected for the protection of liberty and of life.[1]

IN these words, uttered in debate in the House of Representatives in 1831, John Quincy Adams gave classic expression to the theory that the war power is a constitutionally unlimited power.

The *locus classicus* of the opposed doctrine is the opinion of Justice Davis in *ex parte* Milligan,[2] which was decided shortly after the Civil War. The rascally hero of this famous constitutional drama — one of those numerous scoundrels who have contrived to perpetuate their names by the easy device of an appearance in court — was tried in 1864 by Presidential authorization for disloyal practices before a military commission in his home State of Indiana, con-

---

[1] *Register of Debates*, XII, 4037–8.
[2] 4 Wall. 2 (1866).

78

victed, and sentenced to hang. Fortunately or unfortunately, depending somewhat on the point of view, the sentence had not been executed when, with the war ended and the habeas corpus privilege restored, Milligan was enabled to prosecute a petition for his release to the Supreme Court. The justices were unanimously of opinion that the petition should be granted, but parted company as to the grounds of their ruling. Five of them held that the trial, having taken place outside "the theatre of active military operations" and in a region where the civil courts were open, was beyond the power of the Commander-in-Chief to have ordered. The salient passage of Justice Davis's opinion is the following:

> No doctrine involving more pernicious consequences was ever invented by the wit of man than that any of its [the Constitution's] provisions can be suspended during any of the great exigencies of government. Such a doctrine leads directly to anarchy or despotism, but the theory of necessity on which it is based is false; for the government, within the Constitution, has all the powers granted to it, which are necessary to preserve its existence; as has been happily proved by the result of the great effort to throw off its just authority.[3]

These words have been quoted hundreds of times, usually with approval, but, when they are set over against the facts of the case, they become sheer fustian, for as the majority itself held, the Constitution *had* been suspended in Milligan's case, and by none other than Abraham Lincoln, and Milligan's case was but one of hundreds! Four of the justices, headed by Chief Justice Chase, although they found Milligan's trial to have been illegal under provisions of the Act of March 3, 1863, which regulated the suspension of the habeas corpus privilege, yet went on to dispute the majority's constitutional doctrine. Citing Congress's protective power over the forces that it is authorized by the Con-

[3] Ibid., pp. 120–1.

stitution to raise and support, and its power to adopt "legislation essential to the prosecution of war with vigor and success, except such as interferes with the command of the forces and the conduct of campaigns," they asserted it to be within the power of Congress, or temporarily that of the President, in case of "justifying peril," to establish martial law "in times . . . of civil or foreign war," in "localities where the ordinary law no longer secures public safety and private rights." In a word, the Bill of Rights *could* be suspended in wartime if, in the controlling judgment of *Congress,* the war effort and public safety required it.

Present-day constitutional doctrine ordinarily falls somewhere between these two extremes. War does not of itself render constitutional limitations liable to outright suspension by either Congress or President, but does frequently make them considerably less stiff — the war emergency infiltrates them and renders them pliable. Earlier constitutional absolutism is replaced by constitutional relativity; it all depends — a result that has been definitely aided in the case of substantive rights by the modern conception of due process of law as "reasonable law" — that is to say, what the Supreme Court finds to be reasonable in the circumstances.

2

Let us in this connection turn first to those proprietarian and economic interests through its impact upon which total war affects the life of the community most pervasively, and with ever increasing severity as war is prolonged. The constitutional provisions that are of greatest importance in this connection are the two final clauses of Amendment V, which read:

> No person . . . shall be . . . deprived of life, liberty, or property without due process of law; nor shall private property be taken for public use without just compensation.

It was held in 1871 in the Legal Tender cases [4] that the second and more definite of these provisions applied only to direct appropriations of property and hence had no bearing on the exercise of governmental power in wartime simply because of its collateral effect on property values; and today this result holds in the main for any exercise by the National Government at any time of its delegated powers which is otherwise justifiable under the "necessary and proper" clause. As to the "due process" clause, the Court being at that date still unaware that it reached other than procedural questions, dismissed it as irrelevant to the problem of constitutionality raised by the Legal Tender Act. Today the stone thus rejected has become the very head of the column of constitutional law touching private rights; and what it means in relation to the property right is simply this: that the Court is prepared to inquire more or less closely into the factual justification back of any exertion of governmental power which seriously impairs the normal expectancies of ownership.

As was amply demonstrated in World War I, such a limitation on the war power is unlikely to affect its exercise very materially in the presence of the urgencies of total war. The delegations of power to the President made by the Lever Food and Fuel Control Act of August 17, 1917 yield eloquent testimony in this connection: these embraced the power to regulate by license the importation, manufacture, storage, mining, or distribution of necessaries; the power to requisition foods, feeds, fuels, and other necessaries; the power to purchase, store, and sell certain foods; the power to take over factories, packing houses, pipe lines, mines, or other plants, and operate the same; the power to fix a minimum price for wheat; the power to limit, regulate, or prohibit the use of food materials in the production of alcoholic beverages; the power to fix the price of coal and coke

[4] 12 Wall. 457.

and to regulate the production, sale, and distribution thereof.[5] Except for a minor provision none of this legislation was even challenged in court.[6] War Prohibition *was* challenged, however, and was sustained as an exercise of "implied war powers" arising out of the "necessary and proper" clause when taken in connection with "the war powers expressly granted." In respect of these, said Justice Brandeis, "the Fifth Amendment imposes . . . no greater limitations upon the national power than does the Fourteenth Amendment upon state power"; and the validity of State Prohibition laws had become long since a constitutional commonplace.[7]

Another measure challenged and sustained, although by the close vote of five justices to four, was an act of Congress regulating rentals in the District of Columbia, where the war had produced an acute housing shortage. The majority this time frankly invoked the emergency justification that the majority in the Milligan case had so vehemently stigmatized as utterly pernicious. The precedents, said Justice Holmes, "are enough to establish that a public exigency will justify the legislature in restricting property rights in land to a certain [i.e., to a very uncertain] extent without compensation."[8] Justice McKenna speaking for the minority made vehement protest:

> It is asserted, that the statute has been made necessary by the conditions resulting from the "Imperial German War." The thought instantly comes that the country has had other wars with resulting embarrassments, yet they did not induce the relaxation of constitutional requirements nor the exercise of arbitrary power. Constitutional restraints were increased, not diminished. . . . And this careful adjustment

5 Public No. 41, 65th Congress.
6 *United States* v. *Cohen Grocery Co.*, 255 U. S. 81 (1921).
7 *Hamilton* v. *Ky. Distils. Warehouse Co.*, 251 U. S. 146 (1919).
8 *Block* v. *Hirsch*, 256 U. S. 135 (1921).

of power and rights makes the Constitution what it was intended to be and is, a real charter of liberty, receiving and deserving the praise that has been given it as "the most wonderful work ever struck off at any given time by the brain and purpose of man." And we add that more than a century of trial "has certainly proven the sagacity of the constructors, and the stubborn strength of the fabric." [9]

Thus did constitutional absolutism confront constitutional relativity. The latter, nevertheless, made two concessions to the former: first, Justice Holmes indicated that, except for the provision which the act of Congress made in behalf of the owner's right to a reasonable rental of the premises involved, the Court might have been compelled to treat it as a taking of property without just compensation; and secondly, in a later case the Court, again speaking by Justice Holmes, held that a renewal of the act by Congress in August 1921 was invalid under the Fifth Amendment, *the justifying emergency being now at an end.*[10] The power of the Court to take notice of an emergency is, it appears, a two-edged sword, but its anti-government edge descends only after the emergency is over.

Restrictions that today exist on the property right in consequence of our participation in World War II closely approximate those which were imposed in World War I. Let me briefly summarize such restrictions, and their implications for the war power:

> The government has the right to condemn property for its own wartime uses. It can place mandatory orders, and a manufacturer must make what he is told to make, regardless of the fact that he could earn more profits doing something else. The government can commandeer or requisition any private plant it deems essential to our war program. It can in effect fix prices to be paid by itself for products, and the renegotiation authority — by which several billions were re-

9 Ibid., 160.
10 *Chastleton Corp.* v. *Sinclair,* 264 U. S. 543 (1924).

turned to the Treasury first and last — is one of the means. The government absorbs excess profits through taxation. The government controls the flow of raw materials to the manufacturer, thus again limiting what he can earn on his capital. By priorities over transportation it controls the flow of raw materials further. It sets hours of work, fixes wage scales, compels the payment of overtime wages and establishes working conditions. It can withhold manpower from a plant by labeling its product unessential. It dominates the capital market by furnishing on its own terms the vast bulk of war industry financing.[11]

Finally, through OPA the government elbows aside the law of supply and demand with mandates of its own, setting maximum prices and rents, which the Emergency Price Control Act requires only shall be "generally fair and equitable." Yet when in *Bowles* v. *Willingham* — the sole case in which the Court has been asked to pass on any of the legislation just summarized under the Fifth Amendment — an apartment-house owner complained that the rentals allowed her under this formula did not assure her "a fair return" on her property, she was countered by the Court with this statement:

> A nation which can demand the lives of its men and women in the waging of that war is under no constitutional necessity of providing a system of price control on the domestic front which will assure each landlord a "fair return" on his property.[12]

If that is not constitutional relativity, what is it?

The most bizarre chapter on the relation of the war power to proprietarian and kindred interests has, however, nothing to do with acts of the government in either World War I or World War II, but is the result of a remarkable movement that developed in the interval between them for what was called "Universal Conscription" or "Universal

11 Abstracted from one of Mr. Krock's columns in the *New York Times*.
12 321 U. S. 503 at 519–20 (1944).

Mobilization." [13] The movement fed on the professed belief that the representatives of the people (that is, Congress) had been deluded into declaring war against Germany by the great business interests of the country, the unscrupulous managers of which had then proceeded to capitalize on the national misadventure and to wring from the death-pangs of their fellow citizens huge profits. In the final upshot, it was claimed, some twenty-three thousand new millionaires had been created by the war, — one man asserted twenty-nine thousand! It followed by an inevitable inference that if the chief instigation to war, the unholy prospects of profits, could be eliminated, war would be at the same time eliminated, at any rate for the peace-loving American people; and how, it was asked, could the prospect of profits be more certainly removed than by providing for a universal conscription of wealth, to take place automatically upon a declaration of war?

The idea was given a fervid endorsement by President Harding in his Inaugural Address, and was ardently pushed by the influential *Christian Science Monitor;* and numerous bills were introduced into Congress to put the idea into effect. All ultimately foundered, however, on a single constitutional obstacle. Appropriation by the government of substantially all productive property upon the declaration of war would put upon it, it was urged, an impossible financial burden if the requirements of the Fifth Amendment were to be met — an idea that appears naïve enough today in the presence of a 270-billion-dollar national debt and 110-billion-dollar budgets a still recent memory!

The obituary of this curious crusade was written in a joint resolution approved June 27, 1930, which provided for a commission, to consist of six Cabinet members, four Senators, and four Representatives, "to study and consider"

[13] *Hearings before the Committee on Military Affairs; House of Representatives,* 68th Cong., 1st Sess. (March 11, 13, and 20, 1924) .

amending the Constitution of the United States with a view to authorizing Congress to take private property for public use during a war — that is, it would seem, to take it *without compensation*. Possibly the study and consideration are still proceeding; at least no such amendment has been thus far forthcoming. Even so, the notion of universal conscription is a serpent scotched, not killed — as we discover when we view it from the angle provided by the development of military conscription under the Constitution.

3

As I pointed out in my previous lecture, when the Constitution was adopted standing armies were volunteer and professional — though navies were not, as we know from the record of our experience prior to the War of 1812 with British impressments. So when people in 1789 read the constitutional clause that gives Congress the "power to raise and support armies" — which, it should be noted, is a power that operates in peacetime as well as in wartime — they probably thought of an army that would be recruited by voluntary enlistment. The Framers, none the less, were not entirely unacquainted with a type of compulsory military service for limited purposes. I mean service in the militia. Quite logically, therefore, the clause giving Congress the power to raise armies is shortly followed by a clause empowering it "to provide for calling forth the militia to execute the laws of the Union, suppress insurrections, and repel invasions." The last provision traces back, via the early State constitutions, to medieval England, where the militia was a county institution and where the militiaman could be required by the King to serve outside his home county for only one purpose: namely, to repel invasion. And it was for the purpose of repelling invasion that Secretary of War James Monroe urged a draft late in the War of 1812, the first suggestion of this character in our

history. Although thus carefully qualified, the proposal was
assailed by Daniel Webster in the House as an "infamous
expedient," a "horrible lottery," a casting of the "dice of
blood." "That measures of this nature," said he, "should
be debated at all, in the councils of a free government, is
a cause of dismay. . . . A compulsory loan is not to be
compared, in point of enormity, with a compulsory military service." [14] The calculated dawdling of the House
killed the measure.

The partial draft of 1862 was also based by Congress on
the militia clause, being justified as a measure to suppress
insurrection. The Draft Act of 1863, on the other hand,
ignored the State militia organizations, and so had to be
validated under the Constitution by reference to the clause
about raising armies. In fact, justification of the act took a
much wider range. In the two State decisions that attracted
most attention at the time — for the question did not
reach the Supreme Court — the "fundamental right of
self-preservation" was invoked, and the argument offered
that in an emergency imperiling the very existence of the
nation, the powers reserved by the Tenth Amendment "to
the people" became directly available to the National Government.[15]

In the Selective Service Act of 1917 the draft was for the
first time employed to raise forces for service abroad. The
act broke, therefore, with an Anglo-American legal tradition which had been maintained intact since the time of
Edward III, a fact that Mr. Hannis Taylor urged with in-
sistence but ineffectually on the Court's attention in the
Selective Draft Law cases. Supporting an impatient opin-

[14] Claude M. Fuess: *Daniel Webster* (Boston, 1930), I, 168.
[15] Edward McPherson: *History of the Rebellion* (2nd ed., Washington,
1865), pp. 272–4; Carl Brent Swisher: *American Constitutional Development* (Boston, 1943), pp. 292–5; the opinion of the Court in 245 U. S. 366
(1918).

ion by Chief Justice White, the Court unanimously upheld the act, which it rested on Congress's power "to declare war," its power to "raise and support armies," and its power to pass all laws "necessary and proper" to carry those powers into effect.[16] The stress of the argument was on the power "to raise and support armies." Since this, as was pointed out above, is a power that operates in peacetime as well as in wartime, the decision paved the way for the Selective Training and Service Act of September 16, 1940, which anticipated our entrance into World War II by nearly fifteen months. By the same token, it also paved the way for a postwar act of the same character.

But not only has total war served to push military conscription back into peacetime; it has also prompted the suggestion that the principle of conscription be applied to obtain labor for "essential jobs." In the hearings before the House Committee on Military Affairs in 1924, on "Universal Mobilization," Mr. Baruch wanted the proposed measure to include a draft for industrial as well as military purposes, and so did other champions of "Universal Conscription."[17] In the recent war, labor conscription was authorized by the British Parliament three days after the fall of France, and the Dominions promptly followed suit, although, paradoxically, Canada was unable on account of French Quebec's opposition to adopt full military conscription. Upon our own entry into the war parallel measures for the same purpose were introduced in the Senate and House by Senator Austin and Representative Wadsworth respectively, but were heavily frowned upon at the time by the Administration. Nevertheless, on January 11, 1944, the late President in a surprise message to Congress demanded the enactment of "a national service law which, for the duration of the war, will prevent strikes, and, with certain

16 245 U. S. 366.
17 Reference in note 13 above, at pp. 104, 105, 125.

appropriate exceptions, will make available for war production or any other essential services every able-bodied adult in the nation."

Stating that he had received "a joint recommendation for this law from the heads of the War Department, the Navy Department, and the Maritime Commission," the President proceeded to argue the case for the proposal in the following terms:

> The Federal Government already has the basic power to draft capital and property of all kinds for war purposes on a basis of just compensation.
>
> As you know, I have for three years hesitated to recommend a national service act. Today, however, I am convinced of its necessity. Although I believe that we and our allies can win the war without such a measure, I am certain that nothing less than total mobilization of all our resources of manpower and capital will guarantee an earlier victory, and reduce the toll of suffering and sorrow and blood. . . .
>
> When the very life of the nation is in peril the responsibility for service is common to all men and women. In such a time there can be no discrimination between the men and women who are assigned by the Government to its defense at the battle front and the men and women assigned to produce the vital materials essential to successful military operations. A prompt enactment of a national service law would be merely an expression of the universality of this responsibility.
>
> I believe the country will agree that these statements are the solemn truth.
>
> National service is the most democratic way to wage a war. Like selective service for the armed forces, it rests on the obligation of each citizen to serve his nation to his utmost where he is best qualified.[18]

The spokesmen of organized labor at once threw down the constitutional gage. Their central position was that for labor conscription to be analogous to military conscription,

[18] *New York Times,* January 12, 1944.

"the Federal Government would have to nationalize war industry, in order that the conscripted worker might produce under the direct command of his government, with no profits from his labor accruing to private business"; but since the proposed national service act did not include confiscation of war industry, it meant that the conscripts "would be forced by government to work for private profit," which would be precisely the involuntary servitude that is forbidden by the Thirteenth Amendment. As a feature of universal conscription a labor conscription for war purposes would be constitutional, but not otherwise.[19]

The argument seems to me fantastic. I see no reason why the wage-scale should not take as good care of the laborer's financial interests as the price allowed for the plant's output does of its owner's similar interests. To most Americans a labor conscription would be even more objectionable as a feature of universal conscription than it would standing by itself, would appear to put us farther along the road to totalitarianism. Nor do I forget that, from being a purely wartime measure, military conscription has established itself today as a peacetime expedient as well.

The solution of the labor problem in wartime ought to be sought along the guiding lines of Anglo-American legal principles and should grow logically out of peacetime practice. The common law, as developed by the courts of this country, has always condemned strikes against the public interest.[20] In peacetime this should mean at least strikes by public employees, by employees of public utilities, and employees engaged in the production of essential foods and fuels; in wartime it should mean a universal ban on strikes.

---

19 Matthew Woll, communication to the *New York Times*, January 12, 1944.

20 "A strike may be illegal because of its purpose, however orderly the manner in which it is conducted." Justice Brandeis, speaking for the Court in *Dorchy* v. *Kan.*, 272 U. S. 306 at 311 (1926).

Nor would such a ban affect in any wise the prohibition by the Thirteenth Amendment of "involuntary servitude." Liberty is an individual matter; for as Edmund Burke remarks in the *Reflections,* "When men act in concert, liberty is power."

In consequence of adopting too lax a labor policy at the outset of our entrance into the war, Mr. Roosevelt was finally driven by accumulating difficulties to propose an excessively stringent policy. In point of fact, there was little difference in principle between a labor draft and Mr. McNutt's "work or fight" orders, which rested, as we have seen, on the highly questionable theory that when Congress authorized conscription of certain categories of citizens into the military or naval service, it thereby endowed the President with the power to compel those citizens to do anything he might choose to demand of them as an alternative to their being put on the firing line. It seems extremely unlikely that Congress in enacting conscription really intended to clothe the President with any such coercive powers, or to make the Army a penal institution.

4

We come now to the most drastic invasion of civil rights in the United States which this war has evoked, the most drastic invasion of the rights of citizens of the United States by their own government that has thus far occurred in the history of our nation. On February 19, 1942 the President issued an executive order the essential paragraphs of which read as follows:

> Whereas the successful prosecution of the war requires every possible protection against espionage and against sabotage to national-defense material, national-defense premises, and national-defense utilities . . .
> Now, therefore, by virtue of the authority vested in me as President of the United States, and Commander-in-Chief of

the Army and Navy, I hereby authorize and direct the Secretary of War, and the military commanders whom he may
from time to time designate, whenever he or any designated
commander deems such action necessary or desirable, to prescribe military areas in such places and of such extent as he
or the appropriate military commander may determine, from
which any or all persons may be excluded, and with respect
to which, the right of any person to enter, remain in, or leave
shall be subject to whatever restrictions the Secretary of War
or the appropriate military commander may impose in his
discretion.

The Secretary of War is hereby authorized to provide for
residents of any such area who are excluded therefrom, such
transportation, food, shelter, and other accommodations as
may be necessary, in the judgment of the Secretary of War
or the said military commander, and until other arrangements are made, to accomplish the purpose of this order. . . .

I hereby further authorize and direct all executive departments, independent establishments and other Federal agencies, to assist the Secretary of War or the said military commanders in carrying out this Executive order, including the
furnishing of medical aid, hospitalization, food, clothing,
transportation, use of land, shelter, and other supplies,
equipment, utilities, facilities and services.[21]

In pursuance of this order more than 112,000 Japanese
residents of Western States, of whom nearly two out of
every three were natural-born citizens of the United States,
were eventually removed from their farms and homes and
herded, first in temporary camps, later in ten so-called
"relocation centers," situated in the desert country of California, Arizona, Idaho, Utah, Colorado, and Wyoming and
in the delta areas of Arkansas.

It was apparently the original thought of the Administration to rest its measures touching the west-coast Japanese
simply on the general principle of military necessity and
the power of the Commander-in-Chief in wartime; and
viewed as a *temporary* expedient the order of February 19

21 Exec. Order 9066, 7 *Fed. Reg.* 1407.

could have been justified under the Court's decision in 1909 in the case of *Moyer* v. *Peabody*,[22] in which the governor of Colorado was upheld in jailing temporarily a labor leader as a means of bringing a serious labor disturbance to an end. The governor's act, the Court carefully explained, was not *punitory* (as had been that of the military commission in Milligan's case) , but *preventive* merely, and as such it was, in the circumstances, "due process of law." Shaping justification of the order of February 19 to the pattern of this opinion, we need say only that it represented the President's judgment that the war situation on the west coast threatened imminent violence which would be disastrous to the public safety and to our war effort. The good faith of such a judgment being conceded, as no doubt it would have been judicially, the question of its reasonableness would have been, on the basis of *Moyer* v. *Peabody*, irrelevant.

As a matter of fact, before any action of importance was taken on the Presidential order, the order was supplemented by a Congressional resolution passed at the demand of the Secretary of War.[23] By this single-sentence enactment it was made a misdemeanor "to knowingly enter, remain in, or leave prescribed military areas" contrary to the orders of the Secretary of War or of the commanding officer of the area. In short, Congress in a dozen lines adopted by anticipation any order that might be issued in pursuance of the order of February 19. At the same time the President, by further executive order, created the War Relocation Authority (WRA) , a civilian agency, under whose direction the relocation centers were established and conducted, with what degree of skill, success, and compassion there appears still to be considerable dispute.

One way of constitutionally regularizing our Japanese

[22] 212 U. S. 78 (1909) .

[23] March 21, 1942, ch. 191; 56 Stat. 173; U. S. Code (1940 edition) , tit. 18, § 97a.

segregation measures would have been, of course, to get our Japanese fellow citizens declared "enemy aliens," and the Native Sons of the Golden West early launched a movement looking to that end. The great obstacle in the way of their crusade was the decision of the Supreme Court in 1898 in the Wong Kim Ark case,[24] holding that Chinese born in the United States are, under the first section of the Fourteenth Amendment, natural-born citizens. Meeting head-on the issue thus raised, counsel for the Native Sons attacked this ruling as "about the most injurious" the Court ever handed down. I quote from a special dispatch to the *New York Times* of February 21, 1943:

> Mr. Webb told the court [the Ninth Federal Circuit Court of Appeals] that "without committing treason" he believed that that case [*United States* v. *Wong Kim Ark*] was "erroneously decided."
>
> "Are you asking this court to overrule a decision of the Supreme Court?" Judge Curtis D. Wilbur, senior member of the court asked.
>
> "I'm asking the court, as God gives it light and power, to give a correct judgment according to law," the attorney responded. "I am aware that you have sworn to uphold the Constitution, but I am not aware that you have sworn to follow decisions of the Supreme Court whether they are right or wrong in your judgment."
>
> When Mr. Webb asserted that the country had been settled and the government organized by whites, Judge Denman asked:
>
> "How about the Indians?"
>
> The attorney admitted that "ethnologically speaking" there was a theory that "in the misty past" the Mongolian had been an ancestor to the Indian, whereupon the same judge demanded:
>
> "Do you know anybody who disputes it?"
>
> "I contend," Mr. Webb replied, "that the American Indian is not an Asiatic."

---

24 *United States* v. *Wong Kim Ark*, 169 U. S. 649 (1898).

This rather remarkable conversion of a constitutional issue into an ethnological one is reminiscent of the researches of the late Führer's court ethnologists. One such individual, Dintner by name, having demonstrated to his own satisfaction that Christ was an Aryan, found himself confronted with the still more recondite question of the racial origins of the great Chinese sages. The spirit of scientific detachment displayed by Dintner in meeting this issue cannot be sufficiently praised. "In the present state of evidence," said he, "we must preserve on this question an open mind." [25]

But I should not wish to convey the idea that the Wong Kim Ark case settles all phases of the citizenship question. Congress undoubtedly possesses the power to require that American citizens, of whatever ancestry, and whether native-born or naturalized, who are by the laws of the ancestral country its citizens also, take an oath of loyalty to the United States or else be considered to have renounced their American citizenship. [26]

The first case to reach the Court raising the constitutional issue was that of a Japanese-American named Hirabayashi,[27] who had been convicted in a federal court of violating a curfew order of the west-coast commander and also an order to report by a certain date at a so-called civilian control center. Taking advantage of the fact that sentence was imposed under both counts to run concurrently, the Court held that it had only to pass on the validity of the curfew order, which it construed as a measure to prevent espionage and sabotage. The question before the Court, said the Chief Justice, "is not one of Congressional power to delegate to the President the promulgation of the executive order, but whether, *acting in cooperation,* Congress and the

[25] I am indebted for this anecdote to Professor Lawrence Preuss of the University of Michigan.
[26] See on this point *MacKenzie* v. *Hare,* 239 U. S. at pp. 311–12 (1915).
[27] 320 U. S. 81 (1943).

Executive have constitutional power to impose the curfew restriction here complained of." That is to say, in the field of the war power the powers of President and Congress are *merged* powers, or at least the Court will not attempt to draw the line between them when they collaborate, which means practically that Congressional action is subject to indefinite amendment by the President. The only substantial issue raised by the curfew order, the opinion continued, grew out of its discrimination against citizens of Japanese ancestry. Said the Chief Justice on this point, when the order was considered in the light of "the facts and circumstances of the particular war-setting" in which it was adopted — Japanese naval superiority in the Pacific after Pearl Harbor, the consequent exposure of the west coast to invasion at that time, the lessons taught by fifth-column activities in the European theater of war, the pronounced solidarity of west-coast Japanese in recent years, and the dual citizenship of many of them under Japanese law — when all these circumstances were duly weighed, the Court could not say that the discrimination was groundless, could not say, therefore, that it offended the "due process of law" clause of Amendment V.

While the Chief Justice's opinion appears to have had the unanimous approval of the Court, Justices Murphy and Rutledge felt it necessary to safeguard their positions with a qualifying word or two. The former was particularly at pains to assert that a state of war did not suspend "the broad guarantees of the Bill of Rights and other provisions of the Constitution in protecting essential liberties" and in denouncing "distinctions based on color or ancestry" as "inconsistent with our traditions and ideals." And both justices were in apparent agreement that if the constitutional rights of the citizen were to be put under restraint beyond a certain point in wartime, it could be only by a declaration of martial law and in circumstances warranting

such a declaration. The issues thus raised were destined a
year and a half later, when "the Japanese danger" had
waned considerably, to split the Court.

This happened in the Korematsu case,[28] appellant in
which had confessedly violated an order excluding persons
of Japanese ancestry from a defined area and had also failed
to report at an assembly center in the same area. A majority
of the Court, copying the tactic developed in Hirabayashi's
case, professed to find that the only question before it was
the validity of the exclusion order, and this it sustained in
light of the facts existing at the time it was issued. Three
justices dissented, Justice Roberts on the ground that the
real purpose of the seemingly contradictory order (for how
could a person report at an assembly center in an area from
which he was excluded?) to which appellant had been subjected was "to drive all citizens of Japanese ancestry into
Assembly centers" — in short, to effect their imprisonment.
Justices Murphy and Jackson went farther, finding the exclusion orders themselves beyond the constitutional power
of any *civil* authority to put into effect. Only military authority, they asserted, could take such measures, under a
declaration of martial law and a suspension of the writ of
habeas corpus.[29]

[28] 323 U. S. 214 (1944).
[29] This, at any rate, is how I interpret the following passage from Justice Jackson's opinion:

"When an area is so beset that it must be put under military control at
all, the paramount consideration is that its measures be successful, rather
than legal. . . . Defense measures will not, and often should not, be held
within the limits that bind civil authority in peace. No court can require
a [military] commander to act as a reasonable man . . . a commander
focussing the life of a community on defense is carrying out a military program; he is not making law in the sense the courts know that term. He
issues orders, and they may have a certain authority as military commands,
although they may be very bad as constitutional law.

"But if we cannot confine military expedients by the Constitution,
neither would I distort the Constitution to approve all that the military
deem expedient. . . .

Logically, certainly, this position has much to be said for it. What it amounts to is the assertion that unless it was prepared to assume the responsibility of establishing martial law on the west coast, the government was not constitutionally entitled to adopt the measures it did in the case of Japanese citizens there. At least I should unhesitatingly concede Justices Jackson and Murphy this much, that when Congress decided to thrust its oar into the troubled waters of the west-coast racial situation it ought to have taken the time and trouble to throw a few safeguards around the hapless people it was putting under unrestricted military control. The Act of March 21, 1942 is just about the most heartless measure ever enacted by the American Congress; and the decisions sustaining it, in permitting a confusion of military with civil power, expose the constitutional rights of the individual in time of emergency to dangers without precedent. Practically these cases go beyond the doctrine of the minority in Milligan's case, that Congress may in time of war authorize martial law, for while they in effect concede this, they prettify the concession by further permitting Congress to throw over martial law the sanctifying aegis of civil authority.

In a third case, *ex parte Endo*,[30] which was decided the same day as the Korematsu case, the Court salved its conscience by vigorously unholding the right of a Japanese-American girl whose loyalty was conceded by the WRA to a writ of habeas corpus discharging her unconditionally

---

"I should hold that a civil court cannot be made to enforce an order which violates constitutional limitations even if it is a reasonable exercise of military authority. The courts can exercise only the judicial power, can apply only law, and must abide by the Constitution, or they cease to be civil courts and become instruments of military policy.

". . . I do not think they [the courts] may be asked to execute a military expedient that has no place in law under the Constitution. I would reverse the judgment and discharge the prisoner."

[30] 323 U. S. 283 (1944).

from the agency's custody. The right of the authority to detain Japanese-Americans whose loyalty was not yet established (to whose satisfaction established is not indicated) was, however, inferentially conceded. Nor ought it to escape attention that Miss Endo got her release two and a half years after she first filed her petition! Surely the judicial system ought to do better than that even in total war.

It is not entirely irrelevant from the constitutional point of view to raise the question whether the necessity that was invoked by the Court in behalf of the above measures was really substantial. The simple chronology of events affords considerable ground for skepticism. Pearl Harbor occurred December 7, but it was not until six weeks later that the President issued his order and four weeks after that that Congress passed its supporting resolution; and not until nearly six months after Pearl Harbor, was the drastic Civilian Exclusion Order of May 3 promulgated. Was the war emergency on the west coast intensifying meantime? It seems unlikely, even though the Japanese were pressing their conquest of Malaya and the Philippines during the period. What *was* intensifying unmistakably in this interval was anti-Japanese agitation on the west coast, a compound of community hysteria and self-seeking calculation on the part of persons who saw a chance to get hold of valuable Japanese properties for a song of hate. By these agitators the War Department and Congress permitted themselves to be taken into camp, much to their discredit. The defense is offered, to be sure, that a single act of sabotage could have wrought untold damage. No doubt it could have; and so, in the long run, can a single bad precedent. The sober fact is that neither on the west coast nor in the Hawaiian Islands was one single Japanese, citizen or non-citizen, convicted of one single act of sabotage or espionage in the entire course of the war. Had the authorities stopped short with the curfew order of March 24, making violations of it subject to close military detention, every actual necessity would apparently have been met.

5

The Japanese Segregation cases bring the principle of constitutional relativity to the highest pitch yet; but constitutional absolutism has been subsequently revenged in a measure by the decision of February 25 last, in which the Court, by a vote of 6 to 2, held military government to have been illegally imposed on the Hawaiian Islands during the war.[31] Hardly had the last Japanese planes left the skies over Pearl Harbor on that fateful Sunday when Governor Poindexter, invoking Section 67 of the Hawaiian Organic Act of April 30, 1900, issued a proclamation placing the Territory under "martial law," suspending the writ of habeas corpus and conferring on the local commanding General of the Army all his own powers as governor and also "all of the powers normally exercised by the judicial officers . . . of this territory . . . during the present emergency and until the danger of invasion is removed." With the President's approval, given two days later, the regime that the proclamation set up continued with certain abatements from time to time until October 24, 1944.

Section 67 of the Hawaiian Organic Act reads:

> That the governor shall be responsible for the faithful execution of the laws of the United States and of the Territory of Hawaii within the said Territory, and whenever it becomes necessary he may call upon the commanders of the military and naval forces of the United States in the Territory of Hawaii, or summon the posse comitatus, or call out the militia of the Territory to prevent or suppress lawless violence, invasion, insurrection, or rebellion in said Terri-

[31] *Duncan* v. *Kahanamoku, Sheriff; White* v. *Steer,* 90 *Law. Ed. Advance Opinions,* No. 9. The facts of the two cases, while sufficient to raise the legal constitutional issue, are not otherwise of significance. The documentation of the account in the text is from the opinions of the justices.

tory, and he may, in case of rebellion or invasion, or imminent danger thereof, when the public safety requires it, suspend the privilege of the writ of habeas corpus, or place the Territory, or any part thereof, under martial law until communication can be had with the President and his decision thereon made known.

Section 5 of the same act provides "that the Constitution . . . shall have the same effect within the said Territory as elsewhere in the United States." Was Governor Poindexter's interpretation of Section 67 reconcilable with Section 5? That is to say, was the type of "martial law" which his proclamation inaugurated in the Islands permissible under the Constitution? Even if it was permissible at the beginning, did it remain so to the end?

The answer returned to these questions in "the opinion of the Court" by Justice Black offers a perfect illustration of constitutional absolutism. Setting out from the too dogmatic assertion that "the term 'martial law' carries no precise meaning," the opinion winds up by planting on that expression a very precise meaning indeed. This, in brief, is that the only relationship that can constitutionally subsist between the civil power and the military in connection with law enforcement is one in which the latter has the role of an adjunct police taking orders from the former. While the expression "martial law" has sometimes been used to designate this employment of military forces, the attempt to set this use of the term up as an exclusive concept is little more than the arbitrary *sic volo, sic jubeo* of ultimate authority.[32]

Nor does Justice Murphy's effort to piece out his colleague's argument by reviving the formula of the majority

[32] Cf. such outstanding cases as *Martin* v. *Mott,* 12 Wheat. 19 (1827); *Luther* v. *Borden,* 7 How. 1 (1848); *Moyer* v. *Peabody,* 212 U. S. 78 (1909); also Charles E. Fairman: *The Law of Martial Rule* (Chicago, 1930), Chaps. v and vi.

in the Milligan case improve the Court's position materially. There it was stated that "martial law cannot arise from a *threatened* invasion. The necessity must be actual and present; the invasion must be real, such as effectively closes the courts and deposes the civil administration." The meaning intended is that "martial law" is not judicially cognizable as an act of human authority, but only as an occasional ugly supervening fact. It, therefore, never supplants the civil power in consequence of anybody's exercising any judgment in the matter; it springs into existence automatically when the civil power has ceased to exist for the time being. The idea has a mystical tinge. The suggestion that martial law has been confined in the past to situations which totally deprived persons in authority of discretion again flouts the verdict of history and — for recent years, at least — that of opinion.

The Chief Justice, while concurring "in the result," does so for reasons that repudiate entirely the majority's high-flying conceptualism. "Executive action," he remarks, "is not proof of its own necessity"; there must be judicial review. But what sort of judicial review — what is the nature of its task in such a case as this? "I assume," says the Chief Justice, "that there could be circumstances in which public safety requires, and the Constitution permits, substitution of trials by military tribunals for trials in 'civil courts' "; but he adds:

> I find nothing in the entire record which would fairly suggest that the civil courts were unable to function with their usual efficiency at the times these petitioners were tried, or that their trial by jury in a civil court would have endangered good order or the public safety. The Governor of Hawaii and the Chief Justice of the Hawaiian Supreme Court testified to the contrary. The military authorities themselves testified and advanced no reason which has any bearing on public safety or good order for closing the civil courts to the trial of these petitioners, or for trying them in military

courts. I can only conclude that the trials and the convictions upon which petitioners are now detained, were unauthorized by the statute, and without lawful authority.

In brief, whether military government was constitutionally permissible in the Territory of Hawaii throughout the war depended on the facts; and the military itself had failed to show justifying facts in support of their action, even conceding the continued danger after Pearl Harbor of further invasion.

And it is at this point that Justice Burton, speaking for himself and Justice Frankfurter, joins issue with the majority. His argument embraces two main points. In the first place, he emphasizes the unique importance of the Hawaiian Islands in relation to the Pacific war. I quote:

> Once the Islands are visualized as a battle field under actual invasion, threatened with further invasion, and invaluable to the enemy as a base from which to attack the continental United States, the situation is completely changed from that of an ordinary civilian community. Under conditions likely to disregard even the laws of civilized warfare, the island population was threatened with immediate destruction. It thus became necessary to organize and protect that population against imminent danger from bombing, fire, disruption of water and food supply, disease and all the other incidents of modern warfare. The limited area, limited garrison and great isolation of the Islands put a premium on the efficiency of its civilian defense and on the integration of it with the military defense. All activity was subordinated to executive control as the best constitutional safeguard of the civilian as well as the military life.

Secondly, while conceding the desirability of judicial review, he accompanies the concession with a warning against the courts "judging past military action too closely by the inapplicable standards of judicial, or even military, hindsight."

103

Whether or not [he continues] from the vantage post of the present this Court may disagree with the judgment exercised by the military authorities in their schedule of relaxation of control is not material unless this Court finds that the schedule was so delayed as to exceed the range of discretion which such conditions properly vest in the military authorities.

And at the end he puts this poser:

One way to test the soundness of a decision today that the trial of petitioner White on August 25, 1942, before a provost court on a charge of embezzlement and the trial of petitioner Duncan on March 2, 1944, before a similar court on a charge of maliciously assaulting marine sentries were unconstitutional procedures, is to ask ourselves whether or not on those dates, with the war against Japan in full swing, this Court would have, or should have, granted a writ of habeas corpus, an injunction or a writ of prohibition to release the petitioners or otherwise to oust the provost courts of their claimed jurisdiction. Such a test emphasizes the issue. I believe that this Court would not have been justified in granting the relief suggested at such times. Also I believe that this Court might well have found itself embarrassed had it ordered such relief and then had attempted to enforce its order in the theater of military operations, at a time when the area was under martial law and the writ of habeas corpus will still be [*sic*] suspended, all in accordance with the orders of the President of the United States and the Governor of Hawaii issued under their interpretation of the discretion and responsibility vested in them by the Constitution of the United States and by the Organic Act of Hawaii enacted by Congress.

I own that I find this course of reasoning very persuasive, the more so as I take note of the fact that while the Court granted certiorari in these cases on February 12, 1945, it did not get around to deciding them until more than a year later, and I wonder just why this happened. Could it possibly have been because the Court hesitated even at that late date to interpose constitutional difficulties in the way of a possible restoration of military rule in the Islands if the necessity — as judged, of course, by the military — should arise?

At the same time, we are not obliged to endorse everything that was done by the military while the Islands were subject to its sway. The shortcomings of the "military mind," its worship of speed, "toughness," and secrecy, are notorious and they did not fail at times to assert themselves on this occasion. The moment military government was clamped down on the Territory of Hawaii a "curtain of silence" descended between the Territory and the rest of the country; indeed, that curtain has not been entirely lifted even yet. Enough has come to light, none the less, to create a strong suspicion that the military authorities were guilty at times of acts of injustice toward individuals which could not have commended themselves as calculated to advance the general cause to any except minds artificially conditioned against the promptings of common sense and common humanity.[33]

[33] In some of his broadcasts from the Islands directed against the present Advocate General of the Army, Major General Thomas H. Green, who with the rank of colonel was second in command in Hawaii during the war, Mr. Fulton Lewis, Jr., has produced some pretty convincing evidence of gratuitous harshness on the part of Hawaii's military rulers in certain individual cases, and even of a labor draft suggestive of peonage in some parts of the Islands. And we know positively that the Army, early in the war, shipped some thirteen naturalized American citizens to Camp McCoy, Wisconsin, without charges or hearings, and that when it learned that efforts were being made to secure the release of these persons by habeas corpus proceedings, the War Department returned some if not all of them to the Islands. See further: Garner Anthony: "Martial Law in Hawaii," 30 *California Law Review* (January 1942) , pp. 371 ff.; same: "Martial Law in Hawaii," 31 ibid. (December 1943) , pp. 477 ff.; Archibald King: "The Legality of Martial Law in Hawaii," 30 ibid. (September 1942) , pp. 599 ff.; Walter P. Armstrong: "Martial Law in Hawaii," 29 *Journal of American Bar Association* (December 1943) , pp. 698 ff.; John P. Frank: "Ex Parte Milligan *v.* The Five Companies: Martial Law in Hawaii," 44 *Columbia Law Review* (September 1944) , pp. 639 ff.

6

The rights involved in the Japanese Segregation cases and the Hawaiian Martial Law cases were those which are most intimately associated with human personality, the right to secure residence and the right to personal freedom. But freedom of speech and press, too, are valued constitutional rights, and the Court has in recent years lavished a good deal of loving care on them in sustaining the various endeavors of religious enthusiasts and labor picketers to make public nuisances of themselves.[34] The principle of relativity still applies, however. As Justice Holmes phrased the principle during World War I, with reference to the Sedition Act of 1917:

> The character of every act depends upon the circumstances in which it is done. The most stringent protection of free speech would not protect a man in falsely shouting fire in a theatre and causing a panic. It does not even protect a man from an injunction against uttering words that may have all the effect of force. . . . When a nation is at war many things that might be said in time of peace are such a hindrance to its effort that their utterance will not be endured so long as men fight and that no Court could regard them as protected by any constitutional right.[35]

Surveying the effects of World War II on freedom of speech and press down to the end of 1942, Professor Cushman makes a comparison with World War I that is distinctly favorable to our more recent war effort. "Today," he says, "civil liberty enjoys a vitality which even the optimist had hardly dared hope for. There are," he adds, "several reasons for this," of which he enumerates the following:

> First, since the last World War the American people have become "civil liberty conscious." That war found us totally

34 See my *The Constitution and What It Means Today* (8th ed., Princeton, 1946) , pp. 189–91.
35 *Schenck* v. *U. S.*, 249 U. S. 47, 52 (1919) .

unprepared to deal with our sudden problems affecting civil liberty. Our legislatures had no experience in drafting, or our executive officers in enforcing, emergency restrictions upon free speech and press. Our trial courts faced new and difficult civil liberty questions with no established principles, no relevant Supreme Court decisions, to guide them. Since that time, the Supreme Court, in nearly a score of important decisions, has interpreted and strengthened our constitutional civil liberties. . . .

Second, the complete suppression of civil liberty in Axis-controlled countries has been a shocking and impressive object lesson. . . .

Third, we are fighting this war with a real conviction of its necessity. We were attacked. All argument as to *whether* and *when* we should fight was stopped.

Fourth, we have had a centralized federal management of civil liberty problems. The states have wisely refrained from dealing with subversive talk, publications, or conduct. This has permitted the Department of Justice to operate uniformly throughout the country.

Finally, the Administration, through President Roosevelt and Attorney General Biddle, has steadily declared its determination not to repeat the excesses of the government during the last war. The government's record may not be immaculate, but it has followed a positive policy of moderation. . . .[36]

While this was printed in February 1943, successive reports of that generally valuable, although occasionally quite exasperating organization, the Civil Liberties Union, make Professor Cushman's estimate valid for World War II as a whole. But there are one or two points at which this estimate needs to be supplemented and partially qualified.

For one thing, it took thirteen months of actual "shooting war" in 1917–18 to bring Congress to the point of enacting anything at all comparable to Section 2 of the Alien

[36] 37 *American Political Science Review* 49 (February 1943); "War-Time Prosecutions for Speech and Publication" (typescript), American Civil Liberties Union (April 1944).

Registration Act of June 28, 1940, whereby it is made unlawful for any person "to knowingly or wilfully advocate, abet, advise, or teach the duty, necessity, desirability, or propriety of overthrowing or destroying any government in the United States by force or violence," or "to print, publish, edit, issue, circulate, sell, distribute or publicly display any written or printed matter" with such forbidden purpose, and so on.[37] One can imagine that with a Mitchell Palmer at the head of the Department of Justice instead of Francis Biddle, these sweeping provisions could have been treated as furnishing warrant for a considerable crusade against holders of unpopular opinions. Yet it may very well be that it was just because the Act of June 28, 1940 was already on the statute books when war broke that, as Professor Cushman points out, the States kept out of the field.

The thing for which the Administration has been most criticized in the field of freedom of speech and press is something that Professor Cushman does not mention. I mean its withholding data on which an informed opinion could be based, and its lending its sanction now and then to some rather questionable efforts at propaganda in its own behalf.[38] Personally I think criticism on the former score at

[37] U. S. Code (1940), tit. 18, § 10.

[38] The prize example of withholding — and something more serious — is dealt with in the following editorial in the *New York Times* of October 23, 1942:

"*The Tokyo Raid:* Until yesterday the people of this country certainly believed that the April 18 air attack on Japan was carried out without loss of an American plane or an American airman, except for the plane and the crew that were interned in Siberia. The country was encouraged to believe this because of the way in which news of the event was given out. General Doolittle himself said, on May 19, when he was decorated by the President, that not one plane had been shot down and that 'none was damaged to an extent that precluded its proceeding to its destination.' Certainly, to the American public, the words 'its destination' meant a place of safety.

"Yesterday, confronted by the fact that the Japanese Government had made public the names of four American airmen alleged to have participated in the April 18 raid, the War Department admitted that these men

least has been somewhat overdone. Newspaper editors and correspondents are interested parties as to the issue raised, and their complaints that the government is not being frank with the public have always to be taken *cum grano*

were missing and revised the generally believed account of what happened on that occasion. In addition to the plane which was interned in Siberia: 'Several others were involved in forced landings in China' and 'a very few of these planes are carried as missing.'

"Surely it would have been better to have announced these facts before Japan forced their announcement — or, at the very least, to have refrained from statements which encouraged a mistaken impression.

"The practice of withholding bad news, or making good news sound even better than it is, is costing the armed services heavily in loss of public confidence."

Interesting also in the same connection is the following item extracted from a Washington dispatch to the *Times* of July 1, 1942:

"Individual opinion about the United States war effort, particularly opinion which presents what might be thought a 'gloomy' picture or indicates that the program is not running perfectly, is considered censorable if destined for Latin-America, even in a personal letter.

"This ruling by the Postal Section of the Office of Censorship in Washington was recently revealed by refusal to transmit mail to Argentina because the viewpoint of the writer was not optimistic. It was frankly admitted by a spokesman for the Office of Censorship that the letter was returned to the sender, not because of any facts contained in the written material, but because there was a direct statement that the American people would have to make sacrifices to win the war.

" 'Our experts here think the letter was too gloomy to permit it to reach a South American reader,' this spokesman stated in answer to an inquiry from the sender. . . .

"The censorship official explained that the Postal Section had decided that Latin Americans must not be allowed to think there is any weakness whatsoever in the American war effort.

" 'You mean we must appear as mechanically perfect as an automobile assembly line?' he was asked.

" 'That's about it,' he replied. 'It's not good psychological warfare to let them think our productive capacity can't meet every demand. We don't want to emphasize the fact that we are being rationed or that our citizens are making sacrifices in their standard of living.'

"He admitted that refusal to transmit the letter in question was direct censorship of personal opinion, although the note accompanying the letter when it was returned to the sender said that it was being held up because it contained 'defense matters.' "

salis. Yet everybody must agree that throughout a great part of the world during the past decade the importance of what was going on was by no means matched by public knowledge concerning it; and while this condition was not one for which our own government was to any great extent responsible, yet its import for the future of democracy is something to create concern. Democracy subsists on public interest. But the problem that these obvious considerations raise is not one of constitutional law; it is one of political ethics, of a brand of ethics that much of the world no longer accepts.

Nor was it pertinent for Professor Cushman to take account of the proceedings that the Department of Justice instituted early in 1942 to cancel the certificates of naturalization of certain American citizens of enemy-alien ancestry. Two general principles govern such cases. The first is that if the defendant in such proceedings took his oath of naturalization with mental reservations, his certificate can be canceled "for fraud" upon this fact being shown by the government. The second principle is that a citizen naturalized *bona fide* has the same constitutional freedom of utterance and belief that a native-born citizen has — the same right to become a Communist or Fascist or anything else.

In two of the three cases which reached it the Court set aside an order of cancellation on the ground that the government had failed to meet the heavy burden of proof that the statute puts upon it. The general result of these holdings is probably beneficial, but in the earliest one, that of *Schneidermann* v. *United States,* the majority, speaking by Justice Murphy, leans so far backward as almost to do a flip-flop. As Chief Justice Stone points out in his dissenting opinion, "Petitioner testified that at the time of his naturalization he subscribed to the principle of socialism as manifested in the writings of Lenin." How the petitioner succeeded in adjusting in his own mind at the time of his naturalization Lenin's doctrine of change by violence with the principles of the Constitution of the United States is more of a mystery than any mundane tribunal ought to be asked to fathom. Reading through Justice Murphy's opinion for the majority, I can readily understand why somebody invented the quip that "the Supreme Court nowadays dispenses justice tempered by Murphy." [39]

Far more questionable in my opinion has been the persistence of the Department of Justice in pushing the so-called "District of Columbia Sedition Case," professionally known today as *McWilliams* v. *United States*. The indictment, which the department originally obtained from the District Grand Jury as far back as July 23, 1942, charged some twenty-eight persons with *conspiring* to violate the Espionage Act of 1917 and the Sedition Act of June 28, 1940 — specifically that section of the latter which makes it unlawful for any person "with intent to . . . impair . . . the . . . morale" of the armed services.

> (1) to advise, counsel, urge, or in any manner cause insubordination, disloyalty, mutiny, or refusal of duty by any member of the military or naval forces of the United States; or
>
> (2) to distribute any written or printed matter which advises, counsels, or urges insubordination, disloyalty, mutiny, or refusal of duty by any member of the military or naval forces of the United States.[40]

---

[39] *Schneidermann* v. *U. S.*, 320 U. S. 118 (1943); *Baumgartner* v. *U. S.*, 322 U. S. 665 (1944); *Knauer* v. *U. S.*, decided June 10, 1946.

Lincoln certainly did not think that the American way of life contemplated a right in minorities to revolutionize by violence. Said he to John Hay: "We must settle this question now, whether in a free government the minority have the right to break up the government whenever they choose. If we fail it will go far to prove the incapability of the people to govern themselves." Quoted by Lyman Bryson in *Political Science Quarterly*, June 1946, p. 174, from Philip Van Doren Stern's *Life and Writings of Abraham Lincoln* (New York, 1942), p. 122.

[40] U. S. Code, tit. 18, §§ 9 and 11. The account here given is based on

And a superseding indictment, with a revised list of defendants, repeated these charges early in January 1943. Two months later, however, the district court dismissed the indictment so far as the Sedition Act was involved because it alleged offenses prior to the enactment of that statute, and subsequently the government itself decided to abandon the case under the Espionage Act. So as finally brought on April 17, 1944 the trial was based on an indictment handed down the previous January 4, which listed only violations of the Sedition Act alleged to have taken place between June 28, 1940 and shortly following Pearl Harbor.

The government's theory of the case is certainly not lacking in scope and audacity. It is, in brief, that the defendants *conspired* with one another and with the leaders of the Nazi Party in Germany to spread disloyalty and demoralization among the armed services of the United States, to accomplish which baleful purpose they circulated copies of *Mein Kampf, Der Stürmer,* the *Galilean,* and so on — some forty-two publications being listed altogether. And to the same end, it is further alleged, they "organized" and "supported" the Nazi Party in Germany, the Foreign Office of the German Reich, the German-American Bund, and so on — some thirty-six organizations being listed. Thus the conspiracy spanned the Atlantic and embraced two nations, including even the government of one.

The list of thirty defendants finally brought to trial make as queer a kettle of fish as was ever assembled by such means — H. Victor Broenstrupp, who delighted in high-

the indictments and reports of the Civil Liberties Union, especially its mimeographed bulletin on "War-time Prosecutions for Speech and Publication" of April 1944. Several of the defendants resisted removal to the District, but all such efforts except that of Willian Griffin, publisher of the *New York Enquirer,* came to naught. For further interesting details respecting the case see the Washington dispatch of Frederick R. Barkley in the Editorial Section of the *New York Times* of Sunday, December 10, 1944.

sounding aliases, William Dudley Pelley, who one time dreamed of marching on Washington with his "Silver Shirts" and seizing the government, Elizabeth Dilling, who once labeled former Chief Justice Hughes "a pink," and so on. Nor can it be doubted that most of the group had at various times given utterance to and circulated matter which was strongly tinged with hatred of Jews and admiration of the Nazis, and which was harshly critical of the late President and his foreign policies. The President was "a warmonger, liar, unscrupulous, and a pawn of Jews, Communists and plutocrats"; "the Nations opposed to the Axis" planned "to use American lives, money and property to defend their decadent institutions," "the Japanese attack on Pearl Harbor was deliberately invited by the public officials of the United States in order to involve the United States in a war," and so on and so forth.

But the essential question is, did these defendants *conspire with one another and/or with the Nazis to do these things;* and if so, did they do it "with intent to impair . . . the morale" of the armed services, or was it their purpose to influence American opinion more widely? In fact, it is not alleged that a special effort was made to reach the armed services directly; the infection apparently was designed to be spread through and from the public at large. Yet at the very time of these alleged activities American bookstores and libraries were freely circulating *Mein Kampf*. It was being put out by American publishing houses in several translations and college students were being required to read it and take examinations on it; and the suggestion that the Roosevelt Administration invited the attack on Pearl Harbor had been so widely voiced that the Pearl Harbor Investigating Committee noticed it and questioned witnesses about it, finally rejecting it. Furthermore, the fact that two or more persons publish and circulate similar views, even rather peculiar ones, on public questions is by

113

itself very insubstantial evidence of concert, or even of acquaintance, among such persons.

In this connection the attitude to date of the American Civil Liberties Union toward the Sedition case has some relevance. In general it has been a hands-off attitude, which this usually very vocal organization explains as resting in part on the understanding that the government was intending to "offer evidence quite outside the area of opinion, involving the receipt by many of the defendants of funds from the German Government prior to our entry into the War." This statement was made five days before the trial began; if any significant evidence of this character was produced during the ensuing trial, the newspapers were singularly negligent about reporting it.

Finally this question arises: Just how did a District of Columbia court obtain jurisdiction of the case? The first two indictments, since they charged conspiracy to violate the Espionage Act of 1917 (as well as the Sedition Act of 1940), had to allege, because of the dependence of this charge on the Conspiracy Statute, an "overt act" or acts, which it placed in the District, thereby establishing the legal presence there of *all* parties to the conspiracy. But the Sedition Act does not require that the conspiracies that it punishes be authenticated by an "overt act," and the indictment of January 4, 1944 does not allege one in precise terms, but instead asserts sweepingly:

> the Grand Jurors aforesaid, upon their oaths aforesaid, do further present that, as part of said conspiracy and as means and methods of accomplishing the objects thereof, the said defendants and co-conspirators, during the period of said conspiracy, in the District of Columbia and within the jurisdiction of this court and at divers other places throughout the United States, in Germany, and elsewhere would do, and they did, among other things, the following:

Then follow the specifications of the indictment.

So, unless the government can prove not only that the alleged conspiracy existed, but also that it had penetrated the District *prior* to the handing down of the indictment on which the trial is based, the trial court will have been without jurisdiction from the first. Yet the fact is that many if not all of the alleged conspirators owe their presence in the District solely to their having been brought there for trial, some of them from points thousands of miles away. To put the matter bluntly, the trial court got physical jurisdiction of these defendants in the first instance on the basis of indictments that alleged simple, definite overt acts on which the Grand Jury was offered some directly relevant if not extremely impressive evidence, and it has since kept jurisdiction of them by jailing or bailing them, presumably on the assumption that the entire case against them would be established finally. Talk about lifting oneself by one's bootstraps — here is a concrete example! I am reminded of the Vermont farmer who was asked if he believed in baptism by immersion. "Sure," he said, "I've seen it done."

The attempted trial of the "conspirators" *en masse,* after proceeding amid scenes of uproar approaching the dimensions of riot for eight months, in the course of which two or three of the defendants died, finally ended early in December 1944 in a mistrial on account of the death of the presiding judge. According to several subsequent announcements, it is still planned to try the survivors in batches, and meantime a search for further evidence is being carried on in Germany. Unless some turns up, the decision in June 1945 setting aside the conviction at Newark of leading members of the German-American Bund makes the prospect of the government's securing a conviction in this instance that will stick most remote. Meantime, nevertheless, the accused will have had to suffer considerably — from being hauled by the dragnet conspiracy charge to what, for many of them, was a remote part of the country,

from standing the expense of bail, or else from languishing
in jail for an unconscionable time, to say nothing of nervous wear and tear. Justice Holmes pointed out nearly a
quarter of a century ago how dangerous a legal weapon the
conspiracy concept is, and with what care it needs to be
employed if it is not to transgress the constitutional guaranty of a trial by one's neighbors.[41] The same Sixth Amendment, moreover, to which Justice Holmes alludes also requires that an accused "be informed of the nature and cause
of the accusation" against him. That any federal court
should have consented to try anybody under an indictment
so utterly lacking in specifications touching the *when*, the
where, and the *how* of the *essential charge* against him —
in this instance the charge of conspiracy — is really amaz-
ing.

[41] *Hyde* v. *U. S.,* 225 U. S. 347 (1913). Speaking by Justice Holmes in
dissent, four justices rejected the construction of the statutes involved —
what are today Section 88 of Title 18 and Section 103 of Title 28 of the
Code — as transgressing the requirements of Amendment VI of the Constitution that "the trial of crimes shall be held in the State and district where
the crimes shall have been committed." "The overt act," Justice Holmes
declared, "is simply evidence that the conspiracy has passed beyond words
and is on foot when the act is done," and it is incapable of passing "jurisdiction to the place where it is done . . . The defendants never were members
of a conspiracy within a thousand miles of the District in fact," and "the
Constitution is not to be satisfied with a fiction . . . If the government
. . . charges only conspiracy . . . trial ought to be where the conspiracy
exists in fact." Ibid. 384. And, this was said, be it noted, in a case which did
not remotely involve freedom of speech and press. Were I a betting man,
my bet would be that if the question of jurisdiction in the Sedition case
ever reaches the Supreme Court, the present Bench will elect to guide on
Justice Holmes's opinion rather than the Court's opinion in the Hyde case.

  It is unfortunate that the Supreme Court declines to grant applications
for the writ of habeas corpus for the review of removal proceedings, but
leaves the question of the propriety of the removal to the jurisdiction of
the court in which the indictment was found. *Rumely* v. *McCarthy,* 250
U. S. 283 (1919), and cases there cited. The Bundist cases are *Keegan* v.
U. S. and *Kunze* v. *U. S.,* 325 U. S. 478, decided June 11, 1945.

7

Two years earlier, in the summer of 1942, the dramatic Case of the Saboteurs had arisen.[42] Originally there were eight of these gentry, one of them named Haupt being an American citizen, the others citizens of the Third Reich; but subsequently one of the latter turned state's evidence — and then there were seven. The following facts were brought out at the trial: that all of the saboteurs had once lived in the United States; that on the outbreak of war between Germany and the United States all had enrolled for training in sabotage in a school near Berlin which was under the direction of a member of the German High Command; that on the completion of this course they had shipped for this country in two groups on German submarines with instructions to destroy American war industries; that under cover of darkness one group had landed on Long Island, the other on the Florida coast; that both groups had forthwith doffed their German uniforms or parts of uniforms and buried them in the sand, along with a quantity of explosives, arms, and so forth, and had then proceeded inland in civilian dress; that in this disguise all eight were picked up a few days later in New York and Chicago by the FBI, by whom, pursuant to an order from the Attorney General, they had been immediately surrendered to the Provost Marshal of the District of Columbia — that is, to the military arm of the government.

The trial of the saboteurs began on July 9 before a military commission that had been created six days earlier by Presidential proclamation. Early in the proceedings counsel for the accused initiated an effort to file petitions for writs of habeas corpus in behalf of their clients before the District courts and the Supreme Court, and late in the month the Supreme Court consented to hear arguments on

[42] *Ex parte Quirin*, etc., 317 U. S. 1 (July Special Term, 1942).

these applications, which it promptly denied for reasons set forth by the Chief Justice in a thirty-page opinion published three months later.[43]

At the time of its rendition I characterized this opinion as little more than a ceremonious detour to a predetermined goal intended chiefly for edification, a belief in which I have been subsequently vindicated by the Court itself in its more recent decision in General Yamashita's case. Three main contentions were advanced by counsel for the saboteurs, on which the Court passed. The first was that the offense for which the petitioners were being tried — namely, violation of the laws of war by penetrating the defenses of the United States in disguise for the commission of hostile acts — was one unknown to the laws of the United States. The Chief Justice in answer pointed to the Fifteenth Article of War, which provides for a trial by military commission, as well as in other ways, of such offenders or offenses under the law of war as may be by statute thus triable; and to the continuous practice of the military authorities of the United States from the beginning. Evaluated by the principles that are applicable to criminal trials under the Constitution, the answer was startling in basing the liability of defendants on a casual statutory reference to so vague

---

43 The President's proclamation stated that persons engaged in such activities as the saboteurs were, and under such auspices, were denied access to the courts. On this the Chief Justice commented: "But there is certainly nothing in the Proclamation to preclude access to the Courts for determining its application to the particular case." Whatever the intention of the statement in the proclamation, this comment seems to me sound. The Chief Justice then continues: "And neither the Proclamation nor the fact that they are enemy aliens forecloses consideration by the courts of petitioners' contentions that the Constitution and laws of the United States constitutionally enacted forbid their trial by military commission." If my criticism of the Court's opinion is sound, and, indeed, if its own later opinion in General Yamashita's case is sound, then the statement last quoted is unsound.

a concept as "offenses triable by the law of war." Not only would such a charge fail to acquaint the accused with the "nature and cause of the accusation" against him, but the reduction of it to a sufficiently definite offense except by a statute antedating the commission of such offense would be clearly *ex post facto*.

Secondly, the saboteurs contended that because of the President's departure at certain points from the specifications of the Articles of War in his order creating the trial commission, the latter was not a tribunal known to the laws of the United States. This point the Court answered by holding the trial to be within the powers of the National Government and declining to draw the line between the powers of the President and those of Congress in the premises. In other words, the Court held that the Articles of War, which Congress enacts by virtue of a specific delegation of power from the Constitution, were subject to amendment by the President *ad libitum*.

Lastly, the saboteurs insisted that theirs was not a case "arising in the land and naval forces" in the sense of the Fifth Amendment, and that therefore they were entitled to a civil trial in accordance with the requirements of the Fifth and Sixth Amendments. The first proposition the Chief Justice conceded *arguendo*, but then proceeded to cancel the force of the concession by adding that "no exception was necessary to exclude from the operation" of the Fifth and Sixth Amendments cases that "were never deemed to be within their terms," and that the petitioners' cases were of that kind. It was never the intention of the Fifth and Sixth Amendments, the Chief Justice continued, to require that "unlawful enemy belligerents should be proceeded against only on presentment and trial by jury." Nor was Haupt, though a citizen of the United States, in any different case in this respect from the other petitioners,

119

for all alike were enemy belligerents who by entering the country with hostile intent and in civilian garb had violated the usages of war.

This time the Chief Justice did really succeed in formulating a defensible construction of the constitutional provisions to which saboteurs' counsel had appealed, and in accommodating the trial to them. But his very achievement in this respect only throws into higher relief the unallowable assumption on which the entire opinion rests. This is the assumption that the Constitution applied to this case in some *restrictive* sense, though not in the restrictive sense, or senses, given it by defendants' counsel.

I say that this was an unallowable assumption, for consider the factual situation to which the law had to be modeled. The case was not one that touched the rights of civilians in the remotest way, nor the civil rights of military personnel of the United States in the remotest way, nor yet the relations of military personnel with American civilians. Seven of the defendants were enemy aliens, and as such were totally devoid of constitutional status. Indeed, even had they been civilians properly domiciled in the United States at the outbreak of the war, they would have been subject under the statutes to restraint and other disciplinary action by the President without appeal to the courts. In fact, they had entered the country clandestinely in the midst of war as embodied elements of enemy forces, and at the time of trial were in the custody of the military arm of the United States. These saboteurs were *invaders,* their penetration of the boundary of the country, projected from units of a hostile fleet, was in the circumstances of total war *a military operation,* and their capture, followed by their surrender to the military arm of the government, was a continuance of the same operation. The only provision of the Constitution that had any pertinence to their case was Article II, Section II, clause 1: "The President shall be

Commander-in-Chief of the Army and Navy of the United States." It follows that their trial was a pure act of military power into the circumstances attending which the Court had just as much right to inquire as it would have to enjoin the invasion of a foreign country by order of the President, or as it would have to pass on the validity of the proceedings of the United States Senate in an impeachment trial.

The famous case of Major André during the Revolution, to which the Chief Justice makes reference in a footnote, was a perfect, if somewhat pallid, prototype of the Case of the Saboteurs; and four hundred and fifty years farther back was the case of Perkin Warbeck, dealing with which in the seventh volume of his *Reports,* Coke remarks:

> When the pretender Perkin Warbeck invaded England, "being taken in the war, it was resolved by the Justices, that he could not be punished by the common law, but before the Constable and Marshall (who had special commission under the great seal to hear and determine the same according to martial law) that he had sentence to be drawn, hanged, and quartered, which was executed accordingly." [44]

"Being taken in war" — so were the saboteurs.

It was in reliance on the Chief Justice's opinion in the Saboteurs' case that the Court was invited by General Yamashita's counsel to intervene in behalf of their client. Although the invitation did not aid General Yamashita, it stimulated the justices to restudy their position, and in the Chief Justice's opinion of February 4, 1946, the Court beats a complete, as well as completely *silent,* retreat from the doctrines of the earlier opinion.[45] The doctrine of the later opinion is adequately summed up by Justice Rutledge in his dissenting opinion in the following words:

[44] Quoted from Charles E. Fairman, op. cit. in note 32, p. 3, note 9.
[45] *In re* Yamashita, 90 *Law. Ed. Advance Opinions,* No. 8 (decided February 4, 1946).

The difference between the Court's view of this proceeding and my own comes down in the end to the view, on the one hand, that there is no law restrictive upon these proceedings other than whatever rules and regulations may be prescribed for their government by the executive authority or the military and, on the other hand, that the provisions of the Articles of War, of the Geneva Convention and the Fifth Amendment apply.

Justice Rutledge's own position is based on the theory that "the Constitution follows the flag" on all occasions and everywhere except on the field of combat. "There," he concedes, "the maxim about the law becoming silent in the noise of arms applies." Justice Murphy, too, dissented in a characteristic opinion, saying:

> Yamashita was rushed to trial under an improper charge, given insufficient time to prepare an adequate defense . . . and summarily sentenced to be hanged. In all this needless and unseemly haste there was no serious attempt to charge or to prove that he committed a recognized violation of the laws of war. . . .
> To subject an enemy belligerent to an unfair trial, to charge him with an unrecognized crime, or to vent on him our retributive emotions only antagonizes the enemy nation and hinders the reconciliation necessary to a peaceful world.

There may be a trace of exaggeration in this. Whether so or not, it is totally irrelevant to the question of the Court's jurisdiction which was the only question before it.

Personally, I was a bit disappointed when the Court beat a retreat in the matter of the application of General Tomoyuki Yamashita. I had rather hoped that it would stand by its guns until Göring, Hess, Streicher and Co. petitioned it to save their necks from being stretched at the end of some of Prosecutor Jackson's *ex post facto* law doctrines.[46]

---

[46] I have in mind particularly the charge against Göring and his associates that they plotted war. Undoubtedly they did; and undoubtedly Germany was bound by treaty not to wage wars of aggression, exactly the kind

As aftermath of the Case of the Saboteurs came several treason trials, and one of these, *Cramer* v. *United States,* early in 1945 reached the Supreme Court on a question of constitutional interpretation. Cramer was a naturalized

of war that Göring *et al.* plotted. But war in the contemplation of international law is an act of states, and Germany's obligation under the treaties to which she was party was a state obligation. The translation of this obligation into a rule of penal law binding upon her citizens, which is the basis of the charge against them of plotting war, was a legislative act by the occupying powers, and hence *ex post facto* law as to the activities of Göring *et al.* which eventuated in Germany's war of aggression. The Constitution of the United States forbids Congress to pass *ex post facto* laws, but the prerogative of the President as Commander-in-Chief of American forces when occupying enemy territory is not so constricted. What I say above in this lecture regarding General Yamashita's case holds as to American participation in the Nuremberg trials: the only provision of the Constitution that has any bearing on the subject is the one that makes the President Commander-in-Chief of the Army and Navy.

When the United Nations War Crimes Commission was first created, at London in October 1943, its purpose was announced by Lord Simon to be "to investigate war crimes against nationals of the United Nations." After lists of criminals had been prepared, Lord Simon said further, they were to be furnished the apprehending authorities and when apprehended the criminals were to be "turned over to the proper nation for trial." (*American Journal of International Law,* July 1945, pp. 568–9.) In an address which he gave April 13, 1944 before the American Society of International Law, *Justice* Jackson said: "If it is believed that the example (the person marked for punishment) will outweigh the tendency to create among their own countrymen a myth of martyrdom, then let them be executed." But in that case "let the decision to execute them be made as a military or political decision. We must not use the forms of judicial proceedings to carry out or rationalize previously settled political or military policy." *New York Times,* April 14, 1945. It is interesting to compare this statement with the one by *Prosecutor* Jackson in opening the Nuremberg trials. *New York Times,* November 22, 1945.

The Summary of the verdict of the Nuremberg Court (*New York Times,* October 1, 1946) , recites "the main argument of the defense" as follows: "It was contended that no sovereign power had made aggressive war a crime at the time the alleged criminal acts were committed, that no statute had defined aggressive war, that no penalty had been fixed for its commission, and no court had been created to try and punish defenders [offenders?] in these circumstances." This argument the Court purports to answer as follows: "It was said that to punish defendants for the crime of aggressive war was to indulge in ex-post facto legislation abhorrent to the law of all

citizen of German birth who at the time of the invasion of
the saboteurs was residing in New York City. In response to
a cryptic note left under his door, he went to Grand Central Terminal and there found Thiel, one of the invaders
and an erstwhile friend. Subsequently the two men forgath-
ered at restaurants on two occasions, drank together, and
engaged in extended conversation. Both these meetings
were witnessed by two or more FBI agents, and shortly
thereafter, following Thiel's arrest, Cramer was also taken
into custody, tried, and convicted of treason.

Article III, Section 3 of the Constitution reads:

> Treason against the United States shall consist only in
> levying war against them, or in adhering to their enemies,
> giving them aid and comfort. No person shall be convicted
> of treason unless on the testimony of two witnesses to the
> same overt act, or on confession in open court.

The charge against Cramer was, of course, treason by
"adhering to enemies" of the United States. That he had
rendered Thiel certain services was well established by the
evidence; but had he done so for old times' sake or in the
interest of Germany? The jury, adopting the latter view,
brought in a verdict of guilty, which the Supreme Court,
dividing five and four, upset on the ground that the only

---

civilized nations. In the judgment of the Tribunal these contentions ignore
the true nature of international law which is continually developing, adapting itself to the needs of a changing world as the wisdom and experience
of the succeeding generation dictate. The Tribunal has been concerned
with matters of substance and not mere procedure.

"The Hague Convention contains no statement that a breach of its provisions is a crime, nor is any sentence imposed, nor is there any mention of
the court in which offenders will be tried. Yet the acts outlawed in The
Hague Convention are recognized to be crimes as fully as though they had
been expressly defined as such." The answer is entirely misleading. The
Hague Convention does not profess to legislate, but only to codify, and
breach of the rules of war which it lays down were, in many instances at
least, already crimes punishable by court martial. The Case of the Saboteurs
is an illustration.

See also the Preface to this volume.

overt acts testified to by two witnesses each were insufficient to support the charge of treasonable intent. Conceding this, the minority justices held nevertheless that the conviction was constitutional because adequately supported by the evidence as a whole.

The issue raised is obviously that of the significance to be attached to the "overt act" or acts in such a case: must they be sufficient standing by themselves to prove treasonable intent; or is it enough if they bring the treasonable transaction into the open, thus leaving the way for the prosecuting authorities to establish defendant's guilty intention by circumstantial, documentary, or other collateral evidence? That the latter is the view which has most history back of it, and which our courts have generally followed heretofore, is clear.[47] The other theory seems to have been first advanced in an authoritative way by Lord Reading in Sir Roger Casement's case in 1915, in these words:

> Overt acts are such acts as manifest a criminal intention and tend towards the accomplishment of the criminal object. They are acts by which the purpose is manifested and the means by which it is intended to be fulfilled.

And in *United States* v. *Robinson,* which arose in World War I, Judge Learned Hand, quoting Lord Reading, adopted the same view, which has now become the law of the Court.

Thus *Cramer* v. *United States* [48] remakes the law of treason so far as concerns treason by adhering to an enemy of the United States, just as Marshall's famous decision in the

[47] Opinion of the Court, notes 25 and 38. Most of Justice Jackson's learning seems to have been drawn from an elaborate study undertaken at the instance of the Solicitor General, the part of which dealing with the American materials was published in 58 *Harvard Law Review,* 226 ff. While parading much of this learning in lengthy footnotes, the Justice finally concludes: "Historical materials are . . . of little help" — which is quite true so far as his opinion is concerned.

[48] 325 U. S. 1 (1945) . The case was twice argued.

Burr case had remade it one hundred and forty years earlier as to treason by levying war; [49] and the sum total of the two holdings is the near elimination of treason from the calendar of provable crimes under the Constitution. And just as Marshall's opinion scouted history while professing to vindicate it, so does Justice Jackson's, although hardly so impudently or deliberately as did the great Chief Justice's. The crux of Justice Jackson's argument on the historical question is the following passage in his opinion for the Court:

> It [the Philadelphia Convention] adopted every limitation that the practice of governments had evolved or that politico-legal philosophy to that time had advanced. Limitation of the treason of adherence to the enemy to cases where aid and comfort were given and the requirement of an overt act were both found in the Statute of Edw. III, praised in the writings of Coke and Blackstone, and advocated in Montesquieu's *Spirit of Laws*. Likewise, the two-witness requirement had been used in other statutes, was advocated by Montesquieu in all capital cases, and was a familiar precept of the New Testament, and of Mosaic law. The framers combined all of these known protections and added two of their own which had no precedent. They wrote into the organic act of the new government a prohibition of legislative or judicial creation of new treasons. And a venerable safeguard against false testimony was given a novel application by requiring two witnesses to the same overt act.

Unfortunately the final and culminating sentence of this passage is erroneous. The requirement of two witnesses to "the *same*" overt act is taken from the British Treason Trials Act of 1696, where it appears for the first time as an alternative to the requirement of two overt acts, each testified to by one witness.[50] Curiously enough, in the Appendix that he tacks to his dissenting opinion Justice Douglas falls

49 See my *John Marshall and the Constitution* (Yale University Press, 1919), pp. 101–14.

50 David Hutchison: *The Foundations of the Constitution* (New York, 1928), pp. 215–16; 7 and 8 Wm. III, c. 3.

into the same error. At any rate, a mistake shared by both parties could hardly have been determinative of the issue between them!

8

And so much for the direct impact of total war on the constitutional rights of the individual, both the substantive rights of life, liberty, and property and the procedural right of accused persons to a fair trial in the civil courts. I now wish to point out that these rights are also subject in wartime to side blows, glancing blows, through the impairment of the institutions on the essential integrity of which their practical availability vitally depends. Indeed, such blows may be and are almost bound to be even more serious than direct attacks, for while the latter may curtail the rights at which they are directed, indirect impairment may leave them theoretically undiminished, but actually unenforceable and ineffective for any purpose. And the institution on the maintenance of which the security of the constitutional rights of the individual ordinarily depends most immediately is judicial review. Did, then, judicial review suffer any specific impairment during World War II — an impairment that will be likely to survive the war? I think that this question has to be answered in the affirmative for reasons that I shall proceed to make clear as briefly as possible.

The practical effectiveness of judicial review at any particular time as a protection of the expectancies of individuals against the political branches of the government has always fluctuated and will always continue to fluctuate with the doctrines that the Court applies in interpretation of the Constitution. Thus, rights that the Court formerly deemed restrictive of Congress's power under the "commerce" clause it has in recent years cast into the discard. That is a matter of great importance and one I shall deal with in my final lecture. What I have in mind at the present moment is something different. It is the *possibility* of getting the Court to apply its constitutional doctrines, whether favorable or unfavorable, to acts of the political branches which impinge on private interests. It is this *possibility* that certain legislation and certain decisions of the Supreme Court in the course of World War II have impaired.

By the Emergency Price Control Act of January 30, 1942 it is provided that the Emergency Court of Appeals, which the act creates, "and the Supreme Court upon review of the judgments and orders" of the Emergency Court, "shall have exclusive jurisdiction to determine the validity of any regulation or order" of the Price Administrator, and further that "no court, Federal, State or Territorial, shall have jurisdiction or power to restrain, enjoin or set aside any provision of this Act." [51] In *Lockerty* v. *Phillips,*[52] the first case to come before it involving these provisions, the Court found it unnecessary to go farther than to hold that no other court than the Emergency Court had power to "enjoin" orders of the Administrator, and brushed aside the contention of appellants from the Emergency Court that the above quoted provisions withheld "from all courts authority to pass upon the constitutionality of any provision of the Act or of any order or regulation under it." Said the Chief Justice:

> A construction of the statute which would deny all opportunity for judicial determination of an asserted constitutional right is not to be favored.

But in the case of *Yakus* v. *United States,*[53] decided March 27, 1941, this evasion was no longer possible, since this was a criminal prosecution by the United States itself in a dis-

[51] U. S. Code, tit. 50 — War, Appendix — 924 (d) ; Section 204 (d) of the act as passed.
[52] 319 U. S..182 (1945).
[53] 321 U. S. 414 (1944).

trict court of the United States, in which defendant offered
the defense that the Price Control Act as interpreted and
applied in certain orders of the Price Administrator deprived him of property without due process of law. A divided Court, speaking by the Chief Justice, held that the
above quoted provisions of the Price Control Act were
"broad enough in terms to deprive the district court of
power to consider the validity of the administrative regulation or order as a defense to a criminal prosecution for its
violation"; and that this did not deny the defendant his
constitutional rights, since prior to conviction he might,
following a protest to the Administrator, have brought a
suit for injunction in the Emergency Court of Appeals.

Justice Rutledge, speaking for himself and Justice Murphy, vigorously attacked this holding. The dissenting opinion is a lengthy one, but the crux of it appears in the following passages from it:

> It is one thing for Congress to withhold jurisdiction. It is
> entirely another to confer it and direct that it be exercised
> in a manner inconsistent with constitutional requirements
> òr, what in some instances may be the same thing, without
> regard to them. Once it is held that Congress can require the
> courts criminally to enforce unconstitutional laws or stat-
> utes, including regulations, or to do so without regard for
> their validity, the way will have been found to circumvent the
> supreme law and, what is more, to make the courts parties to
> doing so. This Congress cannot do. There are limits to the
> judicial power. Congress may impose others. And in some
> matters Congress or the President has final say under the
> Constitution. But whenever the judicial power is called into
> play, it is responsible directly to the fundamental law and
> no other authority can intervene to force or authorize the
> judicial body to disregard it. The problem therefore is not
> solely one of individual right or due process of law. It is
> equally one of the separation and independence of the pow-
> ers of government and of the constitutional integrity of the
> judicial process, more especially in criminal trials.

And again:

> The procedural pattern is one which may be adapted to
> the trial of almost any crime. Once approved, it is bound to
> spawn progeny. If in one case Congress thus can withdraw
> from the criminal court the power to consider the validity of
> the regulations on which the charge is based, it can do so for
> other cases, unless limitations are pointed out clearly and spe-
> cifically. And it can do so for statutes as well. In short the
> way will have been found to avoid, if not altogether the
> power of the courts to review legislation for consistency with
> the Constitution, then in part at least their obligation to ob-
> serve its commands and more especially the guaranteed pro-
> tections of persons charged with crime in the trial of their
> causes. This is not merely control or definition of jurisdic-
> tion. It is rather unwarranted abridgment of the judicial
> power in the criminal process.[54]

It seems to me difficult to combat this logic. The Emergency Price Control Act, construed as it is in the Yakus case,
breaks over what has always been thought to be the fundamental distinction between the "judicial power" which the
Constitution itself confers on the national courts and their
"jurisdiction," which for the most part it leaves with Congress to assign within, of course, the limits staked out by
the Constitution. Yet who can deny that the Price Control
Act could easily have been hamstrung if everybody subjected to its regulations had been left unrestricted right to
challenge the validity of such regulations and of the act itself as it was interpreted and applied in them? The holding
in the Yakus case throws into even higher light than did the
Japanese Segregation cases the incompatibility between
the requirements of total war and principles thus far
deemed to be fundamental to government under the Constitution. Nor is this all, unfortunately. For as I see it, this
holding cannot be confined in principle to a period of total
war. Certainly nothing in Chief Justice Stone's opinion sup-

[54] U. S. 414 (1944), 468, 483-4.

plies a convincing reason for any such belief in the face of expanding intervention by the government in the nation's industrial life and its expanding reliance on the administrative process.[55]

By way of summary: The early quarrel between the theory that the clauses of the Constitution protective of private rights were suspended by war and the theory that these clauses remained in full sway in war's despite was resolved in World War I in favor of a compromise theory, what I have termed "constitutional relativity"; and except for the anomalous doctrines of the majority in the Hawaiian cases, this compromise has been observed during the recent war. The restrictive clauses of the Constitution are not, *as to the citizen at least,* automatically suspended, but the scope of the rights to which they extend is capable of being reduced in face of the urgencies of war, sometimes even to the vanishing point, depending on the demands of the war. Theoretically these will be determined by the President and Congress, subject to judicial review; actually the Court will not intrude its veto while war is flagrant. Indeed, by the decision in *Yakus* v. *United States,* the citizen may, in a penal prosecution for violating the orders of a war agency, be denied the right even to plead the Constitution. The

[55] Nearly as objectionable is Section 205 (a) of the act, which reads: "Whenever in the judgment of the Administrator any person has engaged or is about to engage in any acts or practices which constitute or will constitute a violation of any provision of section 4 of this Act, he may make application to the appropriate court for an order enjoining such acts or practices, or for an order enforcing compliance with such provision, and upon a showing by the Administrator that such person has engaged or is about to engage in any such acts or practices a permanent or temporary injunction, restraining order, or other order shall be granted without bond." In other words, an injunction must automatically issue on the demand of the Administrator. This feature of the act was observed and enforced by the Court of Appeals for the District of Columbia, July 22, 1943, in the case of *Brown, Administrator* v. *Hecht Co.* Chief Judge Groner dissented, interpreting the word "shall" in the above quoted section to mean "may."

ominous significance of this holding for the postwar Constitution I shall treat in my final lecture against its appropriate background.[56]

56 The following passage in Justice Sutherland's opinion in *United States* v. *Macintosh*, 283 U. S. 605 (1931), while open to criticism at one or two points, is, taken as a whole, a good statement of the conception of the relativity of constitutional rights in wartime:

"To the end that war may not result in defeat, freedom of speech may, by act of Congress, be curtailed or denied so that the morale of the people and the spirit of the army may not be broken by seditious utterances; freedom of the press curtailed to preserve our military plans and movements from the knowledge of the enemy; deserters and spies put to death without indictment or trial by jury; ships and supplies requisitioned; property of alien enemies, theretofore under the protection of the Constitution, seized without process and converted to the public use without compensation and without due process of law in the ordinary sense of that term; prices of food and other necessities of life fixed or regulated; railways taken over and operated by the government; and other drastic powers, wholly inadmissible in time of peace, exercised to meet the emergencies of war."

But, as has been indicated, there comes a time when this type of doctrine must be curtailed, or the Constitution be conceded to have been suspended. Thus from time to time during World War II, and even during "the War before the War," the suggestion was forthcoming from various quarters that it might be necessary to postpone a Presidential or a Congressional election. See, e.g., Mr. Krock's column in the *New York Times* of September 18, 1941. Indeed, it was argued that in this respect the British system, under which there had been no general election since 1935, was much superior to our own. A similar suggestion was made in 1864, to which President Lincoln made reference in his "Election Serenade Speech" of November 10, 1864, in these words:

"It has long been a grave question whether any government not too strong for the liberties of its people, can be strong enough to maintain its existence in great emergencies. On this point the present rebellion brought our government to a severe test, and a presidential election occurring in regular course during the rebellion, added not a little to the strain. . . . But the election was a necessity. We cannot have free government without elections; if the enemy could force us to forego or postpone a national election, it might fairly claim to have already conquered and ruined us."

When the election of 1864 took place, the adversary armies were still in possession of a large part of seven great States, while four others were under military government and the election could not be held within their borders. No comparable condition occurred during World War II or in the emergency preceding it.

IV

Total Peace and the Constitution

ANY student of American constitutional law and theory must have been especially struck by one great difference between the reception given at Washington, and more particularly in the Senate, to the United Nations Charter and that which was extended a quarter of a century ago to the League of Nations Covenant. The Covenant instantly stirred up in many bosoms all kinds of doubts as to the constitutional competence of the treaty-making authority to put the United States into such an organization. The Charter provoked very few such reactions even in the Senate, although some important constitutional difficulties touching the implementation of the Charter were raised, notably by Senators Taft and Bushfield; but these too were got bravely by in due course, as is attested by the United Nations Participation Act of December 20, 1945.[1]

Why this difference? Are United States Senators bigger and better than they used to be? It is possible, for certainly there is always room for improvement in such matters; and of course the political situation was very different in 1945 from what it was in 1919. Still another partial explanation may possibly be found in those enlarged conceptions of the constitutional powers of the National Government which are one result of the New Deal, and even more in an enlarged conception of the adaptability of the Constitution to problems of government in the modern era, all of which

[1] Public Law 264, 79th Congress 1st Session.

had been confirmed and reinforced by the developments of the war itself.

Moreover, in the quarter of a century and more that had elapsed between the final defeat in the Senate of the League of Nations Covenant and the submission to that body of the United Nations Charter, the Supreme Court had on two occasions given its sanction to expansive views of the competence of the National Government in the field of foreign relations. On April 15, 1920, precisely one month after the final destroying vote of the Senate on the Covenant, the Court handed down its decision in *Missouri v. Holland*,[2] in which it sustained the power of the treaty-making authority to enter into a treaty with Great Britain for the protection of migratory game birds passing seasonally from Canada to the United States or vice versa, although the Constitution says nothing about game birds, and also the power of Congress to authorize regulations to make effective the purpose of the treaty and clothe such regulations with penal sanctions. It was evident therefore that the treaty-making power was not deemed by the Court to be materially hampered by the normal allotment of power between the National Government and the States, an implication that it clarified in express words in the Curtiss-Wright case of 1936 and extended to the entire domain of foreign relations under the Constitution. I dealt with this case in my second lecture, but it will be helpful perhaps if I quote again the salient passage from Justice Sutherland's opinion for the Court:

> It results that the investment of the Federal Government with the powers of external sovereignty did not depend upon the affirmative grants of the Constitution. The powers to declare and wage war, to conclude peace, to make treaties, to maintain diplomatic relations with other sovereignties, if they had never been mentioned in the Constitution, would

[2] 252 U. S. 416.

have vested in the Federal government as a necessary concomitant of nationality.[3]

In different words, the United States is as completely sovereign in the field of international relationship as, say, Great Britain and Russia; from which it manifestly follows that if they could enter the United Nations Organization, so could the United States. Otherwise, the paradox would result that the sovereignty of the United States, while theoretically the equal of theirs, was practically less complete, being less capable of forming international relationships; from its very exorbitance, American sovereignty would be self-defeating.[4]

Finally, there can be no reasonable doubt that the Senate to which the Charter was submitted for approval was far less confident of the security of its own position in the constitutional system than was the Senate that rejected the Covenant. The Senate's triumph in 1919 was the most spectacular in its history; but indeed that was its fatal defeat. For as the years wore on and the world seemed to be getting into a worse and worse mess, and the incompetence of the League to deal with the situation became more and more evident, people who always look about for a devil to blame began pointing the finger of reproach at the body that had so lightheartedly assumed responsibility for keeping the United States out of the League, the one great nation with a comparatively detached outlook and hence the one whose participation, it came more and more to be said, was absolutely indispensable. And recently the finger-pointers became vocal and began paraphrasing Cassius' question: "Upon what meat doth this our Senate feed that it is grown so great?" — a question to which answers were not long in forthcoming. Most of these are irrelevant to our purpose,

[3] 299 U. S. 304, at 318.
[4] See the section on "Sovereignty" in my *Constitution and World Organization*, pp. 1–6.

135

but one of them was undoubtedly calculated to make the Senate pause and consider very carefully before planning a lethal blow at the Charter. For it consisted in pointing out that owing especially to the expanded use of the executive agreement device in recent decades a possible alternative route was open to the United States into the United Nations Organization, provided the President and legislative majorities in the two houses of Congress concurred. Thus, for instance, if we were to regard our entrance in June 1934 into the International Labor Office as a precedent, what was to prevent Congress from authorizing the President by joint resolution to accept membership for the United States in the United Nations Organizations without consulting the Senate in its treaty-making capacity? [5]

So, as a successful outcome of the war for the United Nations became an increasing probability toward the end of 1943, the Senate, caught between the juridical situation just adverted to on the one hand and the rising sentiment of the country in favor of American participation in an international organization for the maintenance of peace on the other hand, found itself in a position strongly reminiscent of that in which the Supreme Court was entrapped following the elections of 1936. Furthermore, it was aware that the author of the Court-packing Message of February 5, 1937 was still President. So it decided to put itself straight with the country pronto, which in effect it did by the passage of the Connally Resolution on November 5, 1943 by the overwhelming vote of 85 to 5. The resolution, drafted in the State Department, put the Senate on record as favoring:

> That the United States cooperate with its comrades-in-arms in securing a just and honorable peace.
> That the United States, acting through its constitutional processes, join with free and sovereign nations in the estab-

[5] *Constitution and World Organization*, pp. 31–54.

lishment and maintenance of international authority with power to prevent aggression and to preserve the peace of the world.

That the Senate recognizes the necessity of there being established at the earliest practicable date a general international organization, based on the principle of the sovereign equality of all peace-loving States, and open to membership by all such States, large and small, for the maintenance of international peace and security.

That, pursuant to the Constitution of the United States, any treaty made to effect the purposes of this resolution, on behalf of the Government of the United States with any other nation or any association of nations, shall be made only by and with the advice and consent of the Senate of the United States, provided two-thirds of the Senators present concur.[6]

The resolution was not entirely unambiguous, but the ambiguity was to the disadvantage of Senatorial claims, for what the resolution said literally was that the United States ought to enter an international organization for the maintenance of peace "through its constitutional processes," but that if a treaty was the method selected, it must be made in the way prescribed by the Constitution. For the rest, the resolution was a pledge of good behavior on the Senate's part in case a treaty was submitted to it. Subsequently the Senate lived up to its pledge quite handsomely.

[6] *New York Times,* November 6, 1943. In his Report on the Crimea Conference, delivered before a joint session of Congress on March 1, 1945, President Roosevelt said: "As you know, I have always been a believer in the document called the Constitution," and added that he had "spent a good deal of time educating two other nations of the world . . . that the Charter has to be . . . approved by the Senate of the United States under the Constitution." *Congressional Record,* Vol. 91, Pt. 2, p. 1620 (March 1, 1945). In the prepared text of the speech which was released by the White House prior to its delivery, the President also said " — as will some of the other arrangements made at Yalta." This clause does not appear in the *Congressional Record. American Journal of International Law,* April, 1946, pp. 382–3.

2

The Charter having been ratified, the next thing was to implement it. But by just what method and in what terms was this to be done? Several interesting constitutional problems presented themselves. For while, as we have just seen, the power of the National Government in the field of foreign relations is complete, or sufficiently so, yet this complete power is shared by President, Congress, and Senate. What, then, were to be the respective roles of these three authorities, first in setting up the machinery whereby American participation in the United Nations was to be made effective, and secondly in putting this machinery in operation when occasion should arise?

The first question was disposed of very swiftly when the time came, although at one period it looked as if there might be some difficulty. Mr. John Foster Dulles, Governor Dewey's pundit on foreign relations during the Presidential campaign of 1944, had taken the position, which was reflected in the Republican platform, that the Charter must be supplemented by further international agreement to be laid before the Senate in its treaty-making capacity, and he had later continued to voice this opinion as delegate to the San Francisco Conference, where, moreover, it was espoused by Senator Connally, Chairman of the Senate Foreign Relations Committee and of the American delegation at the Conference.[7] There was just this much to be said for this position: namely, that the Charter itself speaks of "agreements" to be "concluded between the Security Council and member States" or groups thereof; but it does not say that these agreements shall be treaties, and it does not presume necessarily that such agreements would suffice to put the powers of the agreeing governments into operation without supplementary domestic legislation. Nor, to my

7 Arthur Krock, *New York Times*, December 13, 1944.

mind, for reasons which I shall indicate in due course, would such a presumption have been sound in the case of the United States. Fortunately, President Truman, who held the whip-hand in the matter, since he would have had to negotiate the agreements, announced to the press that the terms of American participation in the United Nations would be settled by an act of Congress, not by further supplementary treaties; and that is how it has been settled.[8]

The first and foremost of the purposes of the United Nations is, in the words of the Charter, this one:

> To maintain international peace and security; and to that end to take effective collective measures for the suppression and removal of threats to the peace and the suppression of acts of aggression or other breaches of the peace, and to bring about by peaceful means and in conformity with the principles of justice and international law, adjustment or settlement of international disputes or situations which might lead to a breach of the peace.[9]

In short, the outstanding purpose of the United Nations is to maintain international peace and security by peaceful means if possible, by coercive means if necessary. And it is in the latter connection that the division of power between the President and the Congress becomes of special importance for its bearing on our ability to perform our part in the organization with efficiency, yet without at the same time impairing the democratic character of our own institutions, which we should be reluctant to pay even for international peace and security if it can be avoided. Indeed, one of the chief reasons advanced for joining with other nations in an effort to maintain international peace is recog-

---

[8] Mr. Truman, however, was only announcing a decision that had already been arrived at in Administration circles, as was indicated in Senator Connally's speech of April 11, 1945 before the Washington Rotary Club. James B. Reston in *New York Times,* April 12, 1945.

[9] Charter, Article 1.

nition of the strain to which total war puts democratic institutions.

Of course, the business end of the United Nations, when it comes to exercising coercion in the maintenance of international peace and security, is the Security Council. Let us, then, imagine a situation which, in the opinion of the Council, constitutes a threat to international peace and security and which obstinately resists every peaceable solution — it is at this point that the extraordinary powers of the Council come into play. In the first place, the Council has the right to designate an aggressor nation (Article 39 of the Charter). Then it has the right to call upon the members of the organization to sever all relations, diplomatic, economic, and other, with such aggressor nation (Article 41). But if even these measures prove inadequate in the judgment of the Council, it is then empowered, in the words of the Charter, to "take such action by air, sea or land forces as may be necessary to maintain or restore international peace and security. Such action may include demonstrations, blockade and other operations by air, sea or land forces of members of the United Nations" (Article 42).

The Charter then continues (Article 43):

> All members of the United Nations, in order to contribute to the maintenance of international peace and security, undertake to make available to the Security Council, on its call and in accordance with a special agreement or agreements, armed forces, assistance and facilities . . . necessary for the purpose of maintaining international peace and security.
>
> Such agreement or agreements shall govern the numbers and types of forces, their degree of readiness and general location, and the nature of the facilities and assistance to be provided.
>
> The agreement or agreements shall be negotiated as soon as possible on the initiative of the Security Council. They shall be concluded between the Security Council and mem-

ber states or between the Security Council and groups of member states and shall be subject to ratification by the signatory states in accordance with their constitutional processes.

Also, says Article 45:

In order to enable the United Nations to take urgent military measures members shall hold immediately available national air force contingents for combined international enforcement action. The strength and degree of readiness of these contingents and plans for their combined action shall be determined within the limits laid down in the special agreement or agreements . . . by the Security Council with the assistance of the Military Staff Committee

— a body that is provided for elsewhere in the Charter.[10]

Now, it was out of these provisions that the constitutional problems to which I have referred arise. Put briefly, they were these two: first, whose representative was the representative of the United States on the Security Council really to be — whose orders was he to take — the President's or Congress's; or was he to be autonomous? Secondly, who was to determine for the United States what armed forces our government was to put at the disposal of the Security Council — was the President alone to do this, or was Congress also entitled to have its say in the matter?

The practical values involved, the values that had to be reconciled if possible in the answers to be returned to these questions, I have already indicated. On the one hand was the obvious need for prompt action by the Security Council in the face of an impending aggression; on the other hand was the need for avoiding autocracy, secret diplomacy, more arrangements like those at Teheran, Yalta, and Potsdam. And the first of these values would in all probability be best furthered by making the American delegate the President's representative, or even by making him com-

[10] Charter, Article 47.

pletely autonomous and hence free to make up his mind on the spot without dictation from Washington; the second value argues, equally without question, for some participation by Congress in the guidance of the American delegate.

Some of my audience may recall at this point that the late President Roosevelt dealt with this very subject in his address before the New York Foreign Policy Association late in the 1944 Presidential campaign. Referring to the Security Council as sketched in the Dumbarton Oaks proposals, which on this point are reproduced in detail in the Charter, Mr. Roosevelt said:

> Peace, like war, can succeed only where there is a will to enforce it, and where there is available power to enforce it.
> The Council of the United Nations must have the power to act quickly and decisively to keep the peace by force, if necessary. A policeman would not be a very effective policeman if, when he saw a felon break into a house, he had to go to the town hall and call a town meeting to issue a warrant before the felon could be arrested.
> It is clear that, if the world organization is to have any reality at all, our representative must be endowed in advance by the people themselves, by constitutional means through their representatives in the Congress, with authority to act.
> If we do not catch the international felon when we have our hands on him, if we let him get away with his loot because the town council has not passed an ordinance authorizing his arrest, then we are not doing our share to prevent another world war. The people of the nation want their Government to act, and not merely talk, whenever and wherever there is a threat to world peace.[11]

The parable was engaging, but it shared the fault common to parables. It substituted a misleading simplification of the problem to be met for a solution of it. What, for one thing, is the identifying mark of an "international felon"? We have today a pretty definite idea as to the identity of

[11] *New York Times,* October 23, 1944.

one or two of them in the recent past, but will the question
always be so easy to answer? International felons are not
likely to have had their fingerprints recorded or their pic-
tures displayed in a rogues' gallery, although when Prosecutor Jackson gets through at Nuremberg, this situation
may be altered. What, indeed, is an *international felony?*
The truth is that your international policeman is going to
be required to act under the Charter as *law-maker* as well
as *law-enforcer* — that is, as *both* town meeting and policeman. Moreover, the arrest of a common felon is not likely
to create quite such a ruction in the community as the arrest, or attempted arrest, of an international felon is likely
to — as witness the war just closed. Yet what all this means
is that the *decisions of the Security Council will frequently
involve political considerations and consequences of the
most serious nature;* and this being so, it was impossible to
think seriously of the American delegate on the Council
acting without constant guidance from Washington. What
in fact the suggestion proposed was that the direction of
our foreign policy should be divided between the President
and the delegate, with the lion's share going to the latter
if UN realized its purpose measurably.

In a word, the suggestion was preposterous, and the
United Nations Participation Act entirely ignores it. Sec.
2 (a) of the act, which is the pertinent one, reads:

> The President, by and with the advice and consent of the
> Senate, shall appoint a representative of the United States at
> the seat of the United Nations who shall have the rank and
> status of envoy extraordinary and ambassador plenipoten-
> tiary, shall receive annual compensation of $20,000, and shall
> hold office at the pleasure of the President. Such representa-
> tive shall represent the United States in the Security Coun-
> cil of the United Nations and shall perform such other func-
> tions in connection with the participation of the United
> States in the United Nations as the President may from time
> to time direct.

And paragraph (e) of the same section adds:

> Nothing contained in this section shall preclude the President or the Secretary of State, at the direction of the President, from representing the United States at any meeting or session or any organ or agency of the United Nations.

3

Let me now shift the spotlight to the provision of Article 43 of the Charter, that each member nation of the international organization shall, by an agreement to be ratified "by the signatory states in accordance with their constitutional processes," contribute a definite quota of armed forces to be put at the disposal of the Security Council.

The constitutional question evoked by this provision was really a three-pronged one: first, could the President, simply by virtue of his powers as Commander-in-Chief and organ of foreign relations, enter into such an agreement without invading Congress's "power to declare war"; secondly, if not, could he nevertheless do so on the score of executing the treaty by which the United States would accept UN — the Charter, that is — and which would be, in some sense of the term, "law of the land"; or, thirdly, if not, yet could Congress authorize him to do so without making an unconstitutional delegation of its war-declaring power? For if all these questions had to be answered "no," then fresh recourse must be had to Congress every time the United States was called upon by the Security Council to contribute armed forces to be employed against an "aggressor," *assuming such employment to be tantamount to an act of war.* I shall take up these three aspects of the constitutional question in one-two-three order.

There were those who seemed to be quite clear in their minds that practice under the Constitution had established for the President, by virtue of his capacity as Commander-in-Chief and organ of foreign relations, the right to put any forces of the United States that he may wish to at the disposal of the Security Council, by it to be used as it might determine, whether with or without the backing of a treaty.[12] They pointed out that from an early date Presidents, invoking this dual role, had employed armed forces of the United States, but especially naval forces, to protect against impending violence the lives and property of American citizens abroad, and sometimes wider interests; that such forces had landed on foreign soil to the derogation of the local sovereignty again and again, and had even fought pitched battles and conducted elections there — and all without Congress having had any voice in the matter. And some of them argued that, in view of the great number of such incidents (Mr. James Grafton Rogers lists about one hundred and fifty of them for the period 1811 to 1941), the war-declaring power of Congress must be regarded as having become today little more than the power to announce formally to the world that the United States is at war, a logical inference from which was that it set no limit to the President's power to put American armed forces at the command of the Security Council for the purpose of repressing an aggressor nation; or, in more general terms, that it set no limit to the President's power even in time of peace to dispose the armed forces of the nation in any way that he might judge would best advance American security, whether he thereby ran the risk of precipitating war or not.[13]

12 See a communication in the *New York Times* of November 5, 1944, signed by Messrs. John W. Davis, W. W. Grant, Philip C. Jessup, George Rublee, James T. Shotwell, and Quincy Wright; also the excellent article by Harry Wilmer Jones entitled "The President, Congress, and Foreign Relations," 29 *California Law Review* (July 1941), pp. 565–85.

13 For a list of "incidents" reaching from 1798 to 1941, see James Grafton Rogers: *World Policing and the Constitution* (Boston: World Peace Foundation; 1945), pp. 92–123. Also pertinent for the period 1811 to 1934 is J. Reuben Clark's Memorandum as Solicitor of the Department of State

While it is apparent from what was said in Lecture I that such reasoning was certainly not devoid of force, yet it by no means told the whole story. The vast proportion of the incidents referred to comprised, as just indicated, *efforts to protect definite rights of persons and property against impending violence,* and were defended on that ground *as not amounting to acts of war.* The United States was itself on one famous occasion the scene of a very similar act of "intervention" by Great Britain. This occurred in 1837, when there was a rebellion in Upper Canada, as it was then called, against the mother country. American sympathizers were permitted by our government, despite repeated protests by the British, to furnish the rebels with arms, many of which were shipped across the Niagara River in a small steamer called the *Caroline.* At last the exasperated British commander, taking the law into his own hands, sent a small party across the river, which was then frozen, and these people cut the *Caroline* out of the ice and sank it. The American government of course demanded an apology and reparations from Great Britain, but without avail. Some years later, when as Secretary of State he was carrying on the negotiations that led to the Webster-Ashburton Treaty, Daniel Webster defined the issue raised by the *Caroline* incident as follows: if the danger confronting the British authorities was "instant, overwhelming, admitting of no delay," then their action was a justifiable act of self-defense and not an act of war or a legitimate cause for reclamations. Impaled on that "if" the issue was permitted to shrivel up and blow away.[14]

---

entitled *Right to Protect Citizens in Foreign Countries by Landing Forces* (Government Printing Office, 1912, 1934). The great majority of the landings were for "the simple protection of American citizens in disturbed areas," and only about a third involved belligerent action.

[14] John Bassett Moore: *Digest of International Law* (Washington, 1906), II, 24, 409; VI, 261; VII, 919.

Total Peace and the Constitution

To be sure, such "acts of self-defense" sometimes exceeded this pattern. In 1854 an American gunboat shelled Greytown, Nicaragua, not for the purpose of preventing an act of violence to American interests, but to secure reparations therefor. But the bombardment had no ulterior political purpose, and was later justified by a United States court in a suit brought against the American commander, on the ground that he must be deemed to have acted by authorization of the President in the discharge of the latter's duty as Chief Executive and Commander-in-Chief to protect American lives and property abroad.[15] Then in 1900 President McKinley, without consulting Congress, contributed a considerable American contingent to the forces that went to the relief of the foreign legations in Peking against the Boxers; but again the measure, so far as the United States was concerned, was purely defensive in character and without any ulterior political advantage in view; and the Chinese Imperial government itself agreed with the American government that it did not constitute "war." [16]

Some of the episodes relied upon by the supporters of Presidential prerogative, however, were undoubtedly genuine acts of "political intervention," to utilize Professor John Bassett Moore's rubric for them; but it must be said that for the most part at least they have always been regarded by many Americans as something to be apologized for. One of these was Polk's action early in 1846 in sending American troops into territory in dispute between Mexico and the United States, with the deliberate purpose *and* with the result of precipitating war with that country. Another was President Grant's similar enterprise in 1870 in Santo Domingo, which failed of its purpose because of

---

[15] *Durand* v. *Hollins*, 4 Blatch. 451 (1859). See also J. D. Richardson: *Messages and Papers of the Presidents* (Washington, 1898), V, 284.

[16] Moore, op. cit., V, 478, 479, 482, 500, 502, 507, 508, 510.

Congressional opposition. Another was the first Roosevelt's coup in 1903 when, in his words, he "took Panama." We later paid a handsome *douceur* to Colombia for this affair, and at the time the President's official defenders were not a little put to it to defend it. There is a story to the effect that when the matter was brought before the Cabinet, Attorney General Knox suggested that perhaps he had better prepare an opinion upholding the President's action, but Secretary of War Root objected. "No, no," he exclaimed, "let's not have it said that this beautiful transaction was marred by the least taint of legality!"

And from T. R.'s "Big Stick" policy and the succeeding "Dollar Diplomacy" of Taft and Wilson issued a number of interventions of a more or less political and warlike character in the Caribbean area, which were undertaken without Congress being consulted. The biggest batch of such episodes occurred between 1910 and 1927. In the latter year, in fact, President Coolidge had over five thousand troops in Nicaragua waging what some folks called a "private war." Mr. Coolidge himself heatedly rejected this characterization of what he was doing. "We are not making war on Nicaragua," he asserted piously, "any more than a policeman is making war on passersby." [17] In other words, our armed forces had just as much right to be on Nicaraguan soil as a policeman has to appear on the streets of his home town. Stretch that idea to cover the earth and you get something closely approximating Mr. Roosevelt's parable of the policeman and the international felon.

But what weight are such precedents entitled to? I should

[17] Thomas A. Bailey: *A Diplomatic History of the United States* (New York, 1940), pp. 711–19. When the late Archbishop of Canterbury visited this country in 1935 he created something of a stir by his declaration, apropos of the Italian invasion of Ethiopia: "For the League of Nations to employ force against an aggressor nation is no more war than a baton-charge by the police against a destructive mob is a riot on the part of the police."

say in the first place, that the countries about the Caribbean had come, thanks to the Monroe Doctrine, to constitute a rather special case even before the Civil War.[18] Also, we may fairly note that precedents created by "Dollar Diplomacy" have been latterly pretty much discredited by "good neighbor" policy. They are today under something of a cloud. Finally, the sampling that Presidential advocates gave us of the entire array of precedents was not altogether representative; for there are also certain "counter-precedents," so to speak. I mean cases in which *Presidents asked Congress in its capacity as the war-declaring power* for authority to employ the armed forces for the protection of American interests abroad in situations that they judged might provoke hostile reactions. President Buchanan, in striking contrast to T. R.'s course more than forty years afterward, repeatedly — and vainly — besought Congress for authority to employ the armed forces to protect Americans passing by the Panama, Nicaragua, and Tehuantepec routes on their way to the gold fields of California. But Jefferson, Madison, Jackson, Lincoln, Grant, McKinley, Taft, Wilson, and F. D. R. too are all on record for similar gestures of deference to Congress's power to declare war, not to mention a number of Secretaries of State.[19] Thus the late President was careful to qualify the promises of aid in his "utmost sympathy" message to France of June 14,

[18] See Arthur Krock's column in the *New York Times,* September 7, 1944; also James B. Reston's dispatch in the same journal for September 10, 1944.

[19] Most of the Presidential utterances referred to are conveniently assembled in Albert H. Putney's article on "Executive Assumption of the War Making Power," *National University Law Review* (May 1927), pp. 1–41. See also Moore, op. cit., VII, pp. 162–8. That the power of Congress comprises the power to "declare a general war" and also the power to "wage a limited war" was asserted by the Supreme Court in *Bas* v. *Tingy,* 4 Dall. 37 (1800) and *Talbot* v. *Seeman,* 1 Cr. 28 (1801). The language of the justices in these early cases implies that any act of war, to be entitled to judicial recognition as such, must be ascribed to Congressional authorization.

1940, with the warning: "These statements carry with them no implication of military commitments. Only Congress can make such commitments." [20] What happened to this

20 The following extract from the 3rd revised edition of Clark's *Memorandum* (cited in note 13 above) is interesting in this same connection: "On February 3, 1914, President Wilson by proclamation revoked the previous proclamation of March 14, 1912, making it unlawful to export arms or munitions of war to Mexico. Shortly thereafter, on April 9, 1914, the famous U.S.S. *Dolphin* incident occurred. The facts are briefly these: A squad of men of the Mexican military forces arrested and marched through the streets of Tampico a commissioned officer of the U.S.S. *Dolphin*, together with seven men composing the crew of the whaleboat of the *Dolphin*. Active negotiations took place with Mexico looking to an adequate form of redress, which finally terminated in Huerta's refusal to meet this Government's demand to unconditionally salute the United States flag. Huerta was willing to make the salute on condition that the American Chargé sign a protocol providing for simultaneous salutes from both Mexico and the United States. On April 20, 1914, President Wilson delivered an address at a joint session of the two houses of Congress on 'The Situation in our Dealings with General Victoriano Huerta at Mexico City.' As a part of his remarks, the President said (*Foreign Relations*, 1914, p. 476):

" '. . . I, therefore, come to ask your approval that I should use the armed forces of the United States in such ways and to such an extent as may be necessary to obtain from General Huerta and his adherents the fullest recognition of the rights and dignity of the United States, even amidst the distressing conditions now unhappily obtaining in Mexico.

" 'There can in what we do be no thought of aggression or of selfish aggrandizement. We seek to maintain the dignity and authority of the United States only because we wish always to keep our great influence unimpaired for the uses of liberty, both in the United States and wherever else it may be employed for the benefit of mankind.'

"The following Joint Resolution was approved on April 22, 1941 (38 Stat. L., 770):

" 'In view of the facts presented by the President of the United States in his address delivered to the Congress in joint session on the twentieth day of April, nineteen hundred and fourteen, with regard to certain affronts and indignities committed against the United States in Mexico: Be it

" '*Resolved by the Senate and House of Representatives of the United States of America in Congress assembled,* That the President is justified in the employment of the armed forces of the United States to enforce his demand for unequivocal amends for certain affronts and indignities committed against the United States.

150

warning two months later I shall remind you in a moment.

Stated in the most favorable terms possible for Presidential prerogative, the constitutional question raised by Article 43 of the United Nations Charter boiled down to this: Would an order of the President putting armed forces of the United States at the disposition of the Security Council for the purpose of preventing or repressing an act of aggression by another state or states against a third state be an act of "political intervention" or an act of "self-defense"? By the test yielded by the vast bulk of the precedents we have just been sampling, it would undoubtedly be an act of "political intervention." At the same time, it was hardly to be denied that both the scope given the idea of "self-defense" in some of these precedents and, on the other hand, the daily observed facts of total war make the distinction a tenuous one these days.

Moreover, there was *one* precedent, the creation of the late President himself, which supported automatically almost *any* act that a President of the United States could conceivably do with the armed forces of the United States. I refer to the fifty-destroyer deal with which I dealt in my first lecture. As I there indicated, the only sound view to take of that transaction, which violated at least two statutes, is that it was rendered legal and constitutional *ex post facto* when Congress appropriated money to build the bases the

---

"'*Be it further resolved,* That the United States disclaims any hostility to the Mexican people or any purpose to make war upon Mexico.

"'APPROVED, *April 22, 1914.*'

"On the morning of April 21, 1914, armed naval forces of the United States occupied the port of Vera Cruz, Mexico. On April 28, 1914, the strength of this force was approximately 316 officers and 6,362 men. On April 30, 1914, the United States naval forces formally turned over the port of Vera Cruz to the army, and on May 2, 1914, General Funston established a military government. Plans for evacuation of the United States forces were completed November 23, 1914, at which time the American troops left Mexican territory." Op. cit. (ed. of 1934), pp. 118–19.

sites for which were thus acquired, and by its subsequent enactment of the Lend-Lease Act, which was a kind of extension of the destroyer deal.

4

But what of the suggestion — question two above — that the President would be constitutionally entitled to proceed to implement Article 43 simply on the score of his duty "to take care that the laws be faithfully executed," the Charter being a treaty "made under the authority of the United States" and hence, in some sense, "law of the land"? Can, in other words, the treaty-making power add dimensions to Presidential power in the field of Congressional power, its power, to wit, to declare war? I am of opinion that this question must today be answered "no."

The treaty-making power can undoubtedly create occasions for exercise by the President of his constitutional powers, but it cannot, I contend, augment the power itself, certainly not at the expense of powers that are specifically reserved by the Constitution to Congress. To illustrate: it is undoubtedly within the competence of the treaty-making power to assume for the United States the obligations for a guaranty treaty. (The very first treaty the United States ever entered into, the Alliance of 1778 with France, was a guaranty treaty.) Nevertheless, if the fulfillment of such obligations entails action tantamount to war, Congress and not the President is the department of government that must be first resorted to *unless* we treat as established the broad-gauge view of the President's control of the forces; and if we do that, then no treaty is needed to piece out Presidential prerogative.

It is true that there are a number of casual judicial dicta to the effect that a treaty repeals conflicting provisions of earlier acts of Congress, but I have been able to track down only one case in which it was held that this had actually occurred, and that was a case which, for several reasons, is not entitled to be taken seriously as a binding construction of the Constitution.[21] Today it is the overwhelming verdict of practice, at least, under the Constitution, that no treaty provision which deals with subject-matter falling to the jurisdiction of Congress by virtue of its enumerated powers can have the force of "law of the land" until Congress has adopted legislation to give it that effect.[22]

And this brings us to the third, and final, of the above suggestions or propositions: namely, that Congress could authorize the President to enter into the kind of agreement called for by Article 43 of the Charter, and that an act or resolution to that effect would not, by existing tests, violate the maxim that Congress may not delegate its powers.[23] The

[21] The reference is to *Cook* v. *U. S.*, 288 U. S. 102 (1933). Speaking by Justice Brandeis, the Court held that Section 581 of the Tariff Act of 1922 had been repealed by the Treaty of May 22, 1924 with Great Britain, but that the re-enactment of the same section in 1930 did not repeal the treaty provision involved! The only precedent cited for the proposition that treaties may repeal inconsistent statutes of earlier date is *Whitney* v. *Robertson*, 124 U. S. 190 (1888), where the question was the obverse one: namely, whether an act of Congress had repealed a treaty, and this question was answered in the affirmative. The assertion, too, in the *Cook* case that the treaty involved was "self-executing" is a simple *ipse dixit*. The holding is a prize example of judicial strong-arm methods, for which, I suspect, the Department of State was primarily responsible.

[22] See the excellent discussion of this subject in *Willoughby on the Constitution* (2nd edition, New York, 1929) I, 548–60; also S. B. Crandall: *Treaties, Their Making and Enforcement* (2nd edition, Washington, D. C., 1916), Chaps. xi–xiii.

[23] It was partially on the contrary ground that Congress refused to grant Buchanan the authority to employ armed forces to protect American citizens passing in transit across the Isthmian routes to California and American vessels in the ports of certain Latin-American countries. He combated the argument vigorously. Richardson: *Messages and Papers*, V, 569–70. "This great power [of declaring war] . . . cannot be delegated or surrendered to the Executive." J. Nelson, dissenting in the Prize cases, 2 Bl. 635, 693 (1863). The majority in that case held, however, that the validating act of August 6, 1861 had "operated to perfectly cure" any possible defect of power in the President to do the acts whose validity was in question before the Court. Ibid., p. 671.

proposition was essentially sound, and the Act of December 20, 1945 is premised upon it.

As we saw in Lecture II, the doctrine that Congress cannot delegate its powers in order to exercise them more efficiently and more effectively is today a pretty frail reliance even in the field of domestic legislation, while in the realm of foreign relations it seems to have been dismissed by the Court altogether in recent cases. The truth is that in the latter field the "cognate powers" of the two departments, to use the Supreme Court's expression, are so broad, so indefinite, so overlapping, that the Court could not disentangle them if it wished to, which, of course, it would be necessary for it to do if it were to attempt to say whether Congress had or had not *delegated* power in a particular instance.[24] And it is also true that Congress has from the beginning repeatedly delegated powers to the President to assist him in carrying out a foreign policy, whether his own or Congress's. By the Act of June 4, 1794 President Washington was forthwith "authorized . . . whenever in his opinion the public safety shall require," to lay an embargo upon all vessels both American and foreign in the ports of the United States, and to continue or revoke the same "whenever he shall think proper." If that was not a delegation of power, what would one look like? But only, it may be objected, of Congress's power over commerce, and not of its war-declaring power. Conceding the point, yet why should Congress's power to declare war be so much more sacrosanct than its power over commerce? And this early act has been followed by a whole series of similar ones.[25]

It is pertinent, too, to mention the Act of March 3, 1819 by which the President was "authorized to instruct the commanders of the public armed vessels of the United

[24] *Panama Refining Co.* v. *Ryan*, 293 U. S. 388, 422 (1935); *United States* v. *Curtiss-Wright Export Corp.*, 229 U. S. 304, 322–8 (1936).

[25] See preceding note.

States to subdue, seize, take," and so on, any armed vessel "which shall have attempted or committed any piratical aggression . . . upon any vessel of the United States, or of the citizens thereof, or upon any other vessel." This measure, still on the statute books, testifies both to the theory prevalent at that date regarding the relative powers of Congress and the President over the armed forces in peacetime and to Congress's right to delegate its power to the President.[26]

But the most recent precedent is the most impressive one. I refer to the Lend-Lease Act of March 11, 1941. In the course of the debate in the Senate on this measure Senator Taft summed it up in these words: "This bill is intended to give the President of the United States the right to carry on an undeclared war against Hitler through all the countries of the world that we can subsidize. . . . It would even permit the President . . . to stimulate wars in other parts of the world." That statement was not exaggerative; the act *did* authorize the President to fight wars by deputy at his discretion. If that was not delegating war-declaring power, what would be? [27]

5

Congress's solution of the various constitutional difficulties above set forth is embodied in the following provisions of the United Nations Participation Act:

> The President is authorized to negotiate a special agreement or agreements with the Security Council which shall be subject to the approval of the Congress by appropriate Act or joint resolution, providing for the numbers and types of armed forces, their degree of readiness and general location, and the nature of facilities and assistance, including rights of passage, to be made available to the Security Council on its call for the purpose of maintaining international

[26] U. S. Code, tit. 33, § 382.
[27] See Lecture I, pp. 28–9 above.

peace and security in accordance with article 43 of said Charter. The President shall not be deemed to require the authorization of the Congress to make available to the Security Council on its call in order to take action under article 42 of said Charter and pursuant to such special agreement or agreements the armed forces, facilities, or assistance provided for therein.

There are several significant things about this legislation. First and foremost is the fact of its having been enacted at all, for the consequence of this is that American implementation of the Charter, and hence its ultimately binding interpretation for the United States, is based on the national legislative power, not on the treaty-making power, nor on Presidential prerogative. The second significant feature of the measure is its assertion of the right of Congress to be kept informed regarding both the activities of the United Nations and American participation therein. The assertion follows logically from the premise of legislative implementation. The third feature of significance is the act's requirement that the special agreement or agreements that it authorizes the President to enter into with the Security Council respecting "the number and type of armed forces," etc., to be put at the disposal of the Council shall be submitted for action by Congress; the authorization is strictly *ad referendum*. Finally, the act, without venturing any categorical statement regarding the extent of Presidential prerogative over the armed forces, specifically withholds its approval of any suggestion that this prerogative would be an available recourse beyond the terms of the authorized agreement.[28]

The general theory of the act is that *American participation in the United Nations is a matter for departmental*

[28] Nothing herein contained shall be construed as an authorization to the President by the Congress to make available to the Securtity Council . . . armed forces . . . in addition to the forces . . . provided for in such special agreement or agreements.

collaboration, and not departmental rivalry. From the constitutional point of view this is the sound theory. For what are the facts that the Constitution and our constitutional history thrust upon our attention in this connection? At the risk of retraveling ground already covered, I would sum them up about as follows: the President, by virtue of being a single individual and always Johnny-on-the-spot, by virtue of the constantly recurrent pressure of crises that would not admit of delay, by virtue of certain theories of executive power, first formulated by Alexander Hamilton in 1793 in the famous "Letters of Pacificus," and by virtue of Lincoln's discovery nearly seventy years later of the "Commander-in-Chief" clause — owing to all these factors, added to the creative power of aggressive personalities — the President has come to claim, and has often been able to make the claim good, a quite indefinite prerogative in the sphere of foreign relations.

But Congress too has vast powers that are capable of determining the direction of foreign policy (as witness the Naval War with France in 1798, the War of 1812, the War with Spain in 1898, the annexation of Hawaii the same year, the Panama Tolls Act of 1913, the Neutrality Acts of 1935 and 1937). For Congress is the body that lays and collects taxes for the common defense, that creates armies and maintains navies, although it does not direct them in wartime, that pledges the public credit, that declares war, that defines offenses against the law of nations; and it has the further power "to make all laws which shall be necessary and proper" — that is, which *it* deems to be such — for carrying into execution not only its own powers but all the powers "of the government of the United States and of any department or officer thereof." Finally, its laws made "in pursuance" of these vast powers are "supreme law of the land" and the President is bound constitutionally to "take care that" they "be faithfully executed."

Total War and the Constitution

So we find the constitutional landscape — the portion of it we are interested in — dominated not by a single monolithic power, but by two massive conglomerates of power, one of which, however, the legislative power, was evidently intended originally to be the predominant one, and *is*, in fact, the predominant one when it can put forth its strength in the furtherance of the demands of American public opinion. But that is just the question — can it do this sufficiently well and sufficiently continuously to maintain the position of authority which the Act of December 20, 1945 implicitly claims for it in the determination of American policy in relation to the United Nations?

It is my belief that our participation in the United Nations cannot, under the Act of December 20, be as effective and helpful as it should be without certain internal reforms in Congress for the handling of questions of foreign relations. I suggest two such reforms, without, however, implying at all that there ought not to be others. In the first place the two houses ought by concurrent resolution to create a small Joint Committee on which both major parties should be represented, and to which should be referred automatically all communications from the President regarding our foreign relations. This committee would, of course, render the Senate Foreign Relations Committee and the House Foreign Affairs Committee superfluous. But not only would such a committee greatly facilitate the association of Congress with the President in the conduct of our foreign relations, but its creation would mark a signal step in that reorganization of Congress which its most friendly critics today agree must soon come about if Congress is to recover its due importance in our constitutional system.

Also, the Senate ought to reform radically its rules of procedure for the handling of matters brought before it by its section of the Joint Committee. The Senate still answers to Woodrow Wilson's description of it in 1917, as "the only legislative body in the world which cannot act when its majority is ready to act." In this connection I noticed months ago an Associated Press dispatch from Washington quoting an attack by the House Judiciary Committee on the "two-thirds" rule for Senate approval of treaties. The point was made that this rule had forced Presidents "to enter into executive agreements regarding important foreign affairs." The maintenance of the rule, the report continued, "instead of working to maintain a great power in the Senate is actually taking that power away from the Senate." [29] While this contention has a great deal of force to it, yet the Senate's chosen mode of doing business by unanimous consent is open to still more serious criticism as conducing to executive agreements and to secret diplomacy, of which one type of executive agreement is an ever available instrument. In the field of domestic legislation the unanimous consent procedure — faintly watered down today by the right of two thirds of the Senate, on petition by sixteen members, to limit debate — provides a sort of antidote to its own poison. For every Senator is well aware that he will wish sooner or later to get some pet measure of his own enacted and so cannot afford to stand in the way of similar enterprises of his colleagues being brought to a vote. But in the field of foreign policy no such automatic check operates. It took the Senate twenty-one years to get around to consent to the treaty receding to Cuba the Isle of Pines; and that fiasco was due far more to the practice of doing business by unanimous consent than to the two-thirds rule.

Indeed, recent events furnish an argument for getting rid of this absurd usage that ought to appeal to the corporate pride of the Senate itself. I refer to the recapture by the Senate within the last few months of public attention to its discussions of foreign policy. This happy development is owing to the intelligent effort of certain outstanding

[29] *New York Times,* December 14, 1944.

Senators to give such discussions a constructive and realistic turn, and to it the obstructive possibilities of the "unanimous consent" rule are a standing menace.

However, suppose — what unfortunately is not wildly improbable — that Congress and the Senate fail to put their respective houses in order so that they can make their due contribution to the cause of keeping the United Nations a viable concern. Assuming that American public opinion regarding the United Nations remains fairly stable, then I should say that the thing most likely to happen is the thing that has happened so often in the past, and especially in recent years. The people will turn to the President and, dismissing the question of secret diplomacy as secondary, will ascribe to him the power to act effectively for the carrying out of our obligations to the United Nations, without awaiting the aid or consent of Congress further than that it can be coerced by successive *faits accomplis,* just as it was coerced prior to our entrance into World War II. The supporting constitutional doctrine will be forthcoming; indeed, as I have shown, it already exists.

Yet such an outcome would, to my mind, be definitely disappointing. For it would sacrifice the opportunity that our entrance into the United Nations affords to bring Congress into the constitutional picture in the formulation of foreign policy, a development that may conceivably have several advantages. First, it should be educative not only of Congress but of American public opinion in this vastly important realm of governmental action; secondly, it should be educative also of world opinion in the possibilities of open diplomacy and at the same time afford some assurance against such disastrous commitments as those at Yalta and Potsdam; thirdly, it should operate to render American foreign policy less autocratic in its inception at home and in its effectuation abroad; again, it should favor the rights of small nations, and in so doing promote the erection of

160

legal and institutional controls upon the super-powers; finally, it should aid — at least, it would not frustrate — the establishment of a closer and more dependable co-operation between the President and Congress in this field, as well as in that of domestic policy.

For seventy-five years — from 1823 to 1898 — the Monroe Doctrine kept Presidential adventuring in the diplomatic field in leading strings, and by so doing moderated aggrandizement of the Presidential office. The trusteeship that we have assumed for world peace and security by entering the United Nations furnishes the point of departure for a foreign policy leading to a comparable result, and toward such a result the United Nations Participation Act takes a further step, for it does not trust everything to the casually instructed — often uninstructed — judgment of a single individual, but invokes the active interest of Congress and the American public, something without which any foreign policy is bound in the long run to fail.

6

I now turn to discuss briefly the constitutional aspects of certain existing proposals for amending the Charter, or even for displacing the United Nations by a world state. Article 23 of the Charter reads:

> The Security Council shall consist of eleven Members of the United Nations. The Republic of China, France, the Union of Soviet Socialist Republics, the United Kingdom of Great Britain and Northern Ireland, and the United States of America shall be permanent members of the Security Council. The General Assembly shall elect six other Members of the United Nations to be non-permanent members of the Security Council, due regard being specially paid, in the first instance to the contribution of Members of the United Nations to the maintenance of international peace and security and to the other purposes of the Organization, and also to equitable geographical distribution.

Article 27 further reads:

1. Each member of the Security Council shall have one vote.
2. Decisions of the Security Council on procedural matters shall be made by an affirmative vote of seven members.
3. Decisions of the Security Council on all other matters shall be made by an affirmative vote of seven members including the concurring votes of the permanent members; provided that, in decisions under Chapter VI, and under paragraph 3 of Article 52, a party to a dispute shall abstain from voting.

It follows from these provisions that the United States, the USSR, Great Britain, China, and France have each a veto on all important decisions of the Security Council. And the principal suggestion for amending the Charter is that this veto power be abolished at least as to all situations involving a permanent member as an interested party. Suppose such an amendment should be proposed, would it be within the treaty-making power of the United States to accept it? The argument in the negative invokes, of course, the idea of sovereignty. For the United States, it is contended, to submit itself to the judgment of other governments would be for it to part with its sovereignty.

The chief difficulty raised by this argument grows out of the obscurity that involves its principal term — what does "sovereignty" mean? The fact is that it means several things, depending on — to employ Mr. Bertrand Russell's phrase — the "universe of discourse" in which it is used. Thus in the history of seventeenth- and eighteenth-century political thought "sovereignty" referred more especially to "popular sovereignty" — that is, the right of peoples to determine the forms of government under which they would live. In international law the "sovereignty" of a nation means especially its independence of control by other nations, subject, nevertheless, to the precepts of international law. Finally, the constitutional-law meaning of "sovereignty" is the power of final decision within the framework of government set up by the Constitution.

Can it be said that "sovereignty" in any of the above senses would be sacrificed by the treaty-making power if it accepted for the United States the obligation to abide by decisions of other nations to which it had not itself specifically consented? Fortunately, for present purposes, the question may be simplified. Conceding that American sovereignty in the first two senses would be affected, yet it would not be more seriously affected than would that of other members of the United Nations — more, in fact, than it is already affected by membership in the United Nations in the case of all states except the permanent members of the Council.

The question thus becomes whether the United States would be sacrificing its *constitutional* sovereignty — that is, the power of decision which is lodged by the Constitution within the framework of government set up by it. But this question, too, needs simplification, since almost everybody would be willing to concede that the United States might consent, by the process laid down in the Constitution for its own amendment, to be bound by decisions in which it did no concur. That, however, is not the question with which we started out. This was whether the *treaty-making authority* could accept such an obligation for the United States, and underlying this question is an unstated assumption without whose support the question lacks logical coherence. This is the idea that a *constitutional* obligation attaches to and sanctions the *international* obligation of any treaty or agreement among nations to which the United States is party, and this idea, when stated as a proposition of American constitutional law, is unsound.

The leading cases bearing on the point are the Head Money cases, decided in 1884, and the Chinese Exclusion case, decided in 1889. Admitting in the latter case that an act passed by Congress in 1888 was in flat contravention of express stipulations of the Treaty of 1868 with the Emperor of China, Justice Field, speaking for the Court, said:

> It is not on that account invalid or to be restricted in its enforcement. The treaties were of no greater legal obligation than the act of Congress. By the Constitution, laws made in pursuance thereof and treaties made under the authority of the United States are both declared to be the supreme law of the land, and no paramount authority is given to one over the other. A treaty, it is true, is in its nature a contract between nations and is often merely promissory in effect. Such legislation will be open to future repeal or amendment. If the treaty operates by its own force, and relates to a subject within the power of Congress, it can be deemed in that particular only the equivalent of a legislative act, to be repealed or modified at the pleasure of Congress. *In either case the last expression of the sovereign will must control.*[30]

In short, American constitutional law knows nothing about the *international* obligation of a treaty. So far as it is concerned, a treaty stands on a level with an act of Congress of even date and is, consequently, subject to repeal, just as the latter is, by a later act of Congress. But this is far from signifying, on the other hand, that an act of Congress which, by intention or otherwise, repeals a treaty provision concludes the rights at international law of the other party or parties to the treaty. Dealing with this point in the Head Money cases, Justice Miller wrote: "A treaty is primarily an international compact between independent nations," and depends for its enforcement "on the interest and power of the governments which are parties to it. If these fail its infraction becomes the subject of international negotiations and reclamations" by the disadvantaged state, "which may in the end be enforced by actual war." [31]

[30] 130 U. S. at 600. (My italics).
[31] 112 U. S. at 598.

Total Peace and the Constitution

Thus, *international obligation is one thing, constitutional obligation a different thing*. When it is a question of the former the United States is just as much entitled to determine the extent of its rights and duties at international law as any other sovereign state is, and not a whit more, a situation which the Constitution alters in no wise. Or to state the point in different words, in relation to the international engagements of the United States, Congress stands on precisely the same footing as does Parliament, for instance, in relation to the international engagements of Great Britain. All of which is a logical, if not inevitable corollary of the doctrine that in the field of foreign relations the National Government is a sovereign government and possesses the whole power of the nation.

And, of course, the same manner of reasoning would vindicate the power of the treaty-making authority, or indeed today that of Congress and the President, in accepting for the United States membership in a world state. At this point, however, we encounter the nation of "sovereignty" in a fourth sense. I mean the conception of it as a kind of metaphysical entity that abides within every sovereign state, distinguishing it from every other form of human association, and which is "inalienable." To enter a world state, it is argued, would be for the United States to alienate its sovereignty, which can't be done. Well, either it can be done or it can't. If the latter, then what is there to worry about? If it can, then what becomes of the doctrine of inalienable sovereignty?

But let us take the doctrine more seriously, and ask ourselves what light our own course of history sheds on the theoretical problem it raises. In the period 1787–88 eleven "sovereign" American States entered into what to them was a super-government. Did they then surrender their sovereignty? Calhoun and others, invoking the notion that sovereignty is inalienable, said "no." Yet Calhoun was forced to concede that the government created by the Constitution possessed, or at least exercised, the power to determine as against the States the scope of its own powers. He saved his position by adducing the supposed fact that in the last resort the States were still entitled to leave the Union. When, however, as a result of the Civil War — but only then — the States lost this right, they, on Calhoun's premises, ceased being sovereign.

Applying, then, the test of this doctrine to the hypothetical case under discussion, that of the United States entering a world state, still the United States would not lose its sovereignty if it retained the right to withdraw at any time from the world state; but if, on the other hand, it attempted to withdraw and the attempt failed, then it would have ceased to be sovereign, not indeed by its own act, since by hypothesis sovereignty cannot be alienated, but in consequence of the rise, outside and over it, of a new sovereignty. Sovereignty cannot be alienated — no; for alienation is a legal process, and the law does not reach sovereignty, which is the source of law. But sovereignty can, in fact, be extinguished by the appearance of another sovereignty into which the former sovereignty becomes merged and submerged.

That seems to be the dialectics of the matter. The fundamental obstacle to a world state is, of course, lack of international community of understanding and felt interest. In this connection it is significant that not even the most enthusiastic agitator in favor of world government proposes to confer on such a government powers at all commensurate with those which were conferred on the government created by the Constitution of 1789. It is important, too, to note that the greatest single force promotive of community of feeling in the case of individual nations produces precisely the contrary effect in the case of the world as a whole — I mean *war*. War against a common foe was the greatest single

cause welding the American Colonies into a nation; but as
to the embryonic world community, every war is disrup-
tive, is in effect a civil war. If H. G. Wells — and the other
Welles — could pull off a real war with Mars, the world
state would arrive in no time. There are, nevertheless, at
least two matters as to which the achievement of the Constitutional Fathers in 1789 has some bearing on what the
promoters of world government would like to accomplish
today. The first is the evidence that the former affords of
the overwhelming importance of leadership in such an enterprise. The other is that, while a certain sense of community was indeed the *cause* of the political unification of
the United States in the first instance, yet today our vastly
strengthened sense of community is the *consequence* of that
same political unification and the blessings that it has
brought in its train. World community? — without it there
can never be world government. World government? —
without it there can never be world community.

V

The Postwar Constitution

THE AMERICAN conception of war has always been that it is something arising outside of the normal course of events, something which is violently and arbitrarily projected across it, and which being removed, the normal course of events will resume its customary flow. From this point of view, the constitutional law of war is one thing, the constitutional law of peace another thing, and never the twain shall meet. Illustrations of this point of view occur all down through our history till the other day.

Writing to his friend Cæsar Rodney of Delaware in 1810, Jefferson remarked: "In time of peace the people look most to their representatives; but in war, to the executive solely." [1] The assumption is evident here that the easy descent into Presidential dictatorship in the presence of a war crisis is just as easily reversed once the crisis is weathered. The reader will recall, too, John Quincy Adams's words quoted in a previous lecture: "There are then, in the authority of Congress and in the Executive, two classes of powers altogether different in their nature and often incompatible with each other — war power and peace power."

And a similar implication pervades President Lincoln's famous letter to Erastus Corning and others, penned in 1863 in answer to their protest against military arrests:

> I am unable [said Lincoln] to appreciate the danger apprehended by the meeting, that the American people will by means of military arrests during the rebellion lose the right to public discussion, the liberty of speech and the press, the

1 *Writings* (P. L. Ford, ed., New York, 1892–9) , IX, 272.

law of evidence, trial by jury, and *habeas corpus* throughout the indefinite peaceful future which I trust lies before them, any more than I am able to believe that a man could contract so strong an appetite for emetics during temporary illness as to persist in feeding upon them during the remainder of his healthful life.[2]

"Emetics" — probably not; but suppose it were "spirits." Mr. Lincoln's choice of words is perhaps a little *too* astute.

As a matter of fact, Lincoln turned out to have uttered pretty good prophecy, as such things go. The decision in the Milligan case in 1866 seriously discredited, even as a wartime practice, the measures that Corning and his associates had protested, while the violent revulsion against Presidential pretensions which marked the Reconstruction Era involved results that had not yet been entirely overcome when the first Roosevelt ascended the Presidency *gratiâ Dei*. Even the ante-bellum doctrine of dual federalism still remained an important part of the armory of judicial review and found utterance in a number of once famous cases.[3] The Court was, to be sure, determined to establish the grand result of the war for constitutional law, the restoration of Marshall's conception of the National Governmetn as one resting of its own right "on every foot of American soil"; but it was equally determined that the States should not be crowded to the wall either, that "the federal equilibrium," as it was termed, should not be upset.

Following World War I the time-worn pattern was again brought forth, by that very personable, if not in all respects great and good statesman, the late Warren Gamaliel Harding, who in his Inaugural sent everybody to leafing his dictionary by congratulatorily assuring the country that it had at last returned to "normalcy." Yet that not everybody even

2 *Writings* (Constitutional ed., New York, 1906), VI, 311–24 at 321.
3 E.g., *Texas v. White*, 7 Wall. 700 (1868); *Collector v. Day*, 11 Wall. 113 (1870); Slaughter House cases, 16 Wall. 36 (1873); etc.

at the time fully participated in the new President's faith in the Constitution's continued resiliency is shown by a nearly contemporary utterance of quite different tenor by Mr. Harding's own Secretary of State. "We may well wonder," Mr. Hughes speculated, ". . . whether Constitutional government as hitherto maintained in this Republic could survive another great war, even victoriously waged." [4]

Actually there was no inconsiderable measure of reaction back to prewar constitutional concepts for some years following Mr. Harding's elevation. On the Harding Court laissez-faireism came to new fruition in such decisions as the District of Columbia Minimum-Wage case and *Wolf Packing Company* v. *Court of Industrial Relations*.[5] In Calvin Coolidge the country received and rejoiced in a President who deliberately cast himself in the role of King Log. When, however, Mr. Hoover essayed a similar role in the struggle over the Hawley-Smoot Tariff Act of 1929, many people began to hark back to the good old turbulent times of King Stork as reincarnated in such Presidents as Theodore Roosevelt and Woodrow Wilson.

Now supervened the most momentous, the most unsettling era in the entire history of American constitutional law — the seven and a half years that elapsed between the stock-market collapse of October 1929 and the decision of the Supreme Court on April 12, 1937 sustaining the Wagner Labor Act. The change which the views of a dominant section of the American people regarding the purpose of government underwent during this period was nothing short of revolutionary, and it was accompanied in due course by a corresponding change of attitude toward constitutional values.

The Constitution of 1789, even though not originally de-

---

[4] *New York Times*, June 22, 1920; quoted in C. B. Swisher: *American Constitutional Development* (Boston, 1943) , p. 1.

[5] 261 U. S. 525 (1923) ; 262 U. S. 522 (1923) .

signed as such, early became primarily a Constitution of Rights, and hence structurally a Constitution of checks and balances. As Webster had put the matter in 1834:

> The first object of a free people is the preservation of their liberty; and liberty is only to be preserved by maintaining constitutional restraints and just divisions of political power. Nothing is more deceptive or more dangerous than the pretence of a desire to simplify government. The simplest governments are despotisms; the next simplest, limited monarchies; but all republics, all governments of law, must impose numerous limitations and qualifications of authority and give many positive and many qualified rights. In other words, they must be subject to rule and regulation. This is the very essence of free political institutions. The spirit of liberty is, indeed, a bold and fearless spirit, but it is also a sharp-sighted spirit. . . . It demands checks; it seeks for guards; it insists on securities; it entrenches itself behind strong defences, and fortifies itself with all possible care againt the assaults of ambition and passion. . . . This is the nature of constitutional liberty; and this is our liberty, if we will rightly understand and preserve it.[6]

And when three years later the panic of 1837 stimulated demands that the government come to the assistance of the financial community, President Van Buren rebuked such suggestions with an excellent statement of the conception of governmental function which underlay the Constitution of Rights:

> All communities [said he] are apt to look to government for too much. Even in our own country, where its powers and duties are so strictly limited, we are prone to do so, especially at periods of sudden embarrassment and distress. But this ought not to be. The framers of our excellent Constitution and the people who approved it with calm and sagacious deliberation acted at the time on a sounder principle. They wisely judged that the less government interferes with private pursuits the better for the general pros-

6 *Writings and Speeches* (National Ed., 1903) , VII, 103, 122–3.

perity. It is not its legitimate object to make men rich or to repair by direct grants of money or legislation in favor of particular pursuits losses not incurred in the public service.[7]

The Constitution of the present year of grace, 1946, is by contrast a *Constitution of Powers,* one that exhibits a growing concentration of power in the hands, first, of the National Government; secondly, in the hands of the President and administrative agencies. Nor is the source of this Constitution of Powers at all obscure. It is the *Constitution of World War I pruned of a few excrescences like Presidentially created agencies, "directives," and "indirect sanctions," and adapted to peacetime uses in an era whose primary demand upon government is no longer the protection of rights but the assurance of security.* And, as we have already seen, World War II was largely fought on the home front on the basis of the constitutional law of World War I. So the situation we are faced with today is that for the first time in our history there is, following a great war, no peacetime Constitution to which we may expect to return in any wholesale way, inasmuch as the Constitution of peacetime and the Constitution of wartime have become, thanks to the New Deal, very much the same Constitution.

2

Prior to the New Deal revolution the three main pillars of our peacetime constitutional law, its main structural elements, were: (1) the doctrine or concept of dual federalism; (2) a certain interpretation of the doctrine of the separation of powers; (3) judicial review. I shall now take up each of these in turn, with a view to estimating briefly its continued viability as a check on the political branches of the National Government.

1. In Marshall's conception of the constitutional role of the Supreme Court, that body was the supreme judicial

[7] Richardson: *Messages and Papers of the Presidents,* III, 344.

organ of a supreme government, and its primary duty was to maintain both supremacies. Dual federalism was the contribution of the Court under Taney. Its basic idea was that "the general government" and the States, being both of them "sovereign," faced each other as equals across the boundary line that divided their respective jurisdictions; and to plot that boundary line as occasion arose was the primary business of the Court — indeed, its chief *raison d'être*.[8]

Today not only has this theory been explicitly expelled by the Court from the field of foreign relations, but it has ceased in fact to exert any real influence in the field of domestic legislation. If other proof of this were lacking, the enactment by Congress of the Fair Labor Standards Act of 1938 and its subsequent ratification by the Court would be sufficient. This measure not only prohibits interstate commerce in goods produced by substandard labor, but directly forbids, with penalties, the employment of labor in industrial production for interstate commerce on other than prescribed terms. And in *United States* v. *Darby* [9] this act was sustained by the Court in all its sweeping provisions, on the basis of an opinion by the late Chief Justice which purports to be based, and logically is based, on Chief Justice Marshall's famous opinions in *McCulloch* v. *Maryland* and *Gibbons* v. *Ogden* of a century and a quarter ago.[10]

The total result is that today not only dual federalism but federalism in any sense has ceased to be capable of obstructing through the processes of judicial review the continued centralization of governmental power in the hands of the National Government. If the Constitution still inhibits this outcome it is only by virtue of such limiting

[8] *Ableman* v. *Booth,* 21 How. 506, 520–1 (1859) ; see also 5 How. 504, 573–4 and 588 (1847) .

[9] 312 U. S. 100 (1941) .

[10] 4 Wheat. 316 (1819) ; 9 Wheat. 1 (1824) .

effect as the Court still gives the terms in which specific powers are granted to the National Government in the Constitutional Document, or to specific limitations on such powers. And today, with the scope given the commerce power, the former type of limitation is nothing to be either depended upon or much concerned about. The control over industry recently exerted by the government through priorities and price regulation in the name of the war power could be at any moment reasserted under the "commerce" clause for purposes of social planning.

2. We turn next to the second great structural principle of our constitutional law in the past, the doctrine of the separation of powers. How has it fared at the hands of recent events, and more particularly at the hands of the New Deal and World War II?

In its most dogmatic form the American conception of the separation of powers may be summed up in the following propositions: (1) there are three intrinsically distinct functions of government, the legislative, the executive, and the judicial; (2) these distinct functions ought to be exercised respectively by three separately manned departments of government; which (3) should be constitutionally equal and mutually independent; and which (4), taken together, cover most of the field of governmental power.[11]

Today this entire colligation of ideas has been shattered by three developments in national governmental practice: first, the growth of Presidential initiative in legislation; secondly, the delegation by Congress of legislative powers to the President; thirdly, the delegation in many instances of like powers to so-called "independent agencies" or commissions, in which are merged "the three powers of government" of Montesquieu's postulate. The first two of these developments had already been brought under the

[11] See, e.g., T. M. Cooley: *General Principles of Constitutional Law* (3rd ed., Boston, 1898), pp. 44–6.

New Deal to a pitch not formerly approximated except temporarily during World War I; the third development the Roosevelt Administration resisted and even attempted to nullify in the interest of further concentration of power in the hands of the President, and during World War II it succeeded in doing so within the field of the war power through the creation of WLB, WPB, WMC, OWI, and so on.

When people talk about "Presidential autocracy" they are apt, especially under war conditions, to be thinking chiefly of those powers which the President receives from the Constitution directly. Actually, as we have seen, a large proportion of the great powers that the President exercises even in wartime are the immediate donation of Congress. The reassurance afforded by this fact turns out on examination, nevertheless, to be meager. For the truth is that the practice of delegated legislation is inevitably and inextricably involved with the whole idea of governmental intervention in the economic field, where the conditions to be regulated are highly complex and are constantly undergoing change. In this situation it is simply out of the question to demand that Congress should attempt to impose upon the shifting and varied scene the relatively permanent molds of statutory provision unqualified by a large degree of administrative discretion.

Nor, by the same token, can the President's role in the formulation of legislation for Congressional consideration be reasonably expected ever to become less than it was during the recent war. One of the major reasons urged for governmental intervention is furnished by the need for gearing the different parts of the industrial process with one another for a planned result. In wartime this need is freely conceded by all; but its need in peacetime is conceivably even greater, inasmuch as the results sought are so much more diversified and complex.

So, in the interest both of unity of design and of flexibility of detail, Presidential power today takes increasing toll from both ends of the legislative process — both from the formulation of legislation and from its administration. In short, the principle of the separation of powers as a barrier preventing the fusion of Presidential and Congressional power is today in an extremely enfeebled condition. And, as I have pointed out in previous lectures, the Court in the course of World War II repeatedly declined to draw the line between Congressional and Presidential power, thus leaving the acts of the former in such instances subject to indefinite amendment by the latter.

3. Finally, let us see what has happened to judicial review in recent years within the theater of national power. Considered as a restraining agency vis-à-vis political power, judicial review has always been a function of constitutional law, its scope and efficacy being directly dependent on the Court's interpretation of the Constitution, and especially of the broader principles that were supposed to underlie it. Thus, in returning to the Marshall conception of national supremacy on April 12, 1937, the Court then and there divested itself of the most potent single weapon it has ever wielded in limitation of national legislative power, the doctrine that there are certain State powers discoverable by the Court itself, which stand on a level with and hence set bounds to national legislative power. Today it requires no gift of prophecy to foresee that never again will the Court hold an act of Congress that is constitutionally unobjectionable in all other respects to be a violation of the Constitution because of its infringing State power. And meantime the "due process" clause has undergone a corresponding impairment. Indeed, it is hardly too much to say that the word "liberty" in the clause has absorbed from the New Deal ideology an equalitarian connotation that transforms it into a positive instigation to projects of social reform.

And inevitably this impairment has been aggravated, as we saw especially in the Japanese Segregation cases, by the compulsive urgencies of total war.

Indeed, in total war the Court necessarily loses some part of its normal freedom of decision and becomes assimilated, like the rest of society, to the mechanism of the national defense. Sometimes it is able to put on a stately parade of judicial clichés to a predetermined destination, but ordinarily the best it can do is to pare down its commitments to a minimum in the hope of regaining its lost freedom in quieter times. Unfortunately in modern conditions the beneficent intention of such efforts is being constantly frustrated by the increasing tendency of society to breed crises, which are often quite as disabling to normal social process as war itself. This is attested, in fact, by the recognition that present-day constitutional law accords "emergency" as a justification for unusual interventions by government, especially in the fields of economic and industrial relations. The first time that the Supreme Court, at least to my knowledge, ever took cognizance of an emergency short of war or invasion as affording such a justification was in the case of *Wilson* v. *New*,[12] in which it sustained, early in 1917, the Adamson Act compelling the railroad companies to grant a wage increase to their employees in order to prevent a nation-wide tie-up of transportation, and even this recognition was made in the face of threatened war. But of the legislative accomplishment of the New Deal, "emergency" was the very watchword, while of the decisions sustaining that legislation it was the recurrent premise, sometimes frankly avowed, sometimes speciously disavowed.[13]

Yet war, public war, total war, is still, no doubt, *the* emer-

[12] 243 U. S. 332.
[13] Compare in this connection the opinions of the Court in the Minnesota Moratorium case, 290 U. S. 398 (1934), and *Stewart Machine Co.* v. *Davis*, 301 U. S. 548 (1937).

177

gency *par excellence;* and it was on this justification, as we saw in Lecture III, that Congress took away from persons prosecuted for violation of the Emergency Price Control Act the right to plead the unconstitutionality of the act or of orders issued under its supposed authorization. Such defendants, said the Court in *Yakus* v. *United States*,[14] were not denied "due process of law," since they could file a protest with the Price Administrator, and following that a suit in the Emergency Court, in which the constitutional question could be raised and from whose decisions an appeal lay to the Supreme Court itself. Conceding the correctness of this holding so far as the "due process" clause is concerned, still it does not answer, or even notice, the objection that in requiring the national courts to decide penal cases without taking the Constitution into account, Congress had obviously invaded the very core of "judicial power," the power and duty of deciding cases in accordance with the standing law of which the Constitution is a part, and an irrepealable part.

In short, judicial review as a restraint on the political branches of the National Government has become impaired in recent years in consequence of the dismissal by the Court, in the course of sustaining the New Deal, of those doctrines which more than any others had enabled it in the past to control Congressional power; on account of the expanded conception in constitutional law of "emergency" as a justification for legislative interference with private freedom of action; on account, finally, of the unexampled disparagement sustained in *Yakus* v. *U. S.* of the distinction between "jurisdiction," which in the case of the national courts Congress *is* entitled to regulate, and "judicial power," which these courts theoretically receive from the Constitution itself, and which has heretofore been gener-

14 See ante pp. 44–5, 128–31.

ally deemed to be beyond the reach of serious legislative curtailment. And this is to pass by with the mere mention of it the belief which some of the present justices appear to share that judicial review is inconsistent with the notion of popular rule.[15]

To repeat, it appears that *our participation in World War II, far from cutting athwart the prevalent trend in constitutional interpretation in peacetime, has simply intensified, extended and accelerated it,* so that we cannot reasonably expect any pronounced reaction from most of the war's results for constitutional law. And what are these results? I would summarize them as follows: (1) the attribution to Congress of a legislative power of indefinite scope; (2) the attribution to the President of the power and duty to stimulate constantly the positive exercise of this indefinite power for enlarged social objectives; (3) the right of Congress to delegate its powers *ad libitum* to the President for the achievement of such enlarged social objectives, which, however, is today qualified by the right to recover such powers through the "concurrent resolution" device and so without first securing Presidential approval; (4) the attribution to the President of a broad prerogative in the meeting of "emergencies" defined by himself and in the creation of executive agencies to assist him; (5) a progressively expanding replacement of the judicial process by the administrative process in the enforcement of the law — sometimes even of constitutional law. Here, in outline, is the postwar constitution or a close approximation of it.

3

A student of mine recently asked me if I did not consider that the Constitution was "on the way out." As the question seemed to be more the inspiration of an idle moment than

15 "Judicial review, itself a limitation on popular government. . . ." Justice Frankfurter in 310 U. S. 586, 600 (1940) .

of serious concern, I answered it according to its author's frivolity. I said that I was reminded of the story of a doctor who was being constantly pestered by a patient with "a heart condition" as to the latter's life expectancy. Finally the medic hit upon a formula that was at once soothful and reasonably truthful. "My dear man," said he, "you can rely upon it, your heart will last as long as you do." Then applying my allegory, I continued to my interlocutor: "You may rely upon it that as long as there is a political entity called the United States of America, it will have *a* Constitution — the only alternative being anarchy and hence the end of entity."

But the question is capable of being put seriously and deserving of a serious answer. Its evident reference is to the Websterian conception of a "Constitution of Rights," featured especially by an elaboration of checks and balances. Obviously, this conception of the Constitution is not only on the way out — it *is* out. Yet unquestionably there were values underlying this conception which we should not wish to see squeezed out of the Constitution altogether, one of them — the most important and most ancient one — being the idea of *liberty against government.*

Is there any way by which this can be kept a viable element of a "Constitution of Powers"? With the minimization of the role of judicial review in the national theater, undoubtedly our principal reliance for this purpose must be a better organization of the relationship of President and Congress; nor may such reorganization have the maintenance of individual rights for its primary objective. Rather, that must come as an incidental result of an arrangement which, by tying the achieved legislative leadership of the President to the leadership of Congress, will constitute something of a guarantee that important legislation will always represent a widespread opinion that it was needed and meritorious, and conversely that projects which do not have that support will fail. *Individual rights cannot rely in this period of our history upon governmental stagnation for their protection.* Their only safeguard, in the long run certainly, is to be found in such constitutional arrangements as best promise that necessary things be done in time, but that the judgment that they are necessary be as widely representative as possible.

For the rest, we must face the fact that the survival among us of constitutional government and the humane values it was meant to conserve depends on many other things than constitutional arrangements, even the most fortunate. Within the last thirty years total war, domestic crisis, new ideologies, and more recently science have conspired to confront our political and juristic tradition with a challenge such as it has never before been required to face. For good or ill we have chosen to "walk the hot plowshares of international politics"; we have invented the atomic bomb and used it against civilian populations, thereby creating a great new problem not only of international security, but of security for our own people; we have legislated into existence nation-wide labor combinations that are able to subject great communities to a state of siege for indefinite periods; our public men from President down have repeatedly held forth the notion that "economic independence and security" for everybody are within the competence of government to provide; on the plea of war necessity we have assembled the most numerous bureaucracy since the Roman Empire, and now that the war is over, appear to be unable or unwilling to reduce it materially; we have contracted a national debt that approaches, if it does not overtop, the total expenditures of all governmental units in the United States prior to World War II. Nor is this to mention the cancerous "race problem" — a misnomer, if ever there was one, since a *problem* is characteristically something that has a *solution*.

Total War and the Constitution

I dislike to end on so portentous a note. Yet surely the first requisite to a solution of difficulties is recognition of their seriousness. In the present case, as in all others in which conditions challenge men's courage and intellectual candor, Bishop Butler's famous words, spoken two centuries ago, remain applicable: "Things and actions are what they are and the consequences will be what they will be; why, then, should we desire to be deceived?"

Index

i

Index

White, C.J., quoted or cited, 36, 88
Willoughby (W. W.) *on the Constitution,* 153n
Wilson v. *New,* 177
Wilson, Woodrow: war labor policy, 48–9, 51; created precedents for war effort in World War II, 49–50, 55, 77; "Dollar Diplomacy" of, 148; orders bombardment of Vera Cruz, 150–1n
WLB, 48–9, 50, 55
WMC, "directives" of, 56–8
Wong Kim Ark case, 94, 95

world state, constitutional possibility of American entry, 162–6
World War I: legislation in, 38ff., 81–3; as rehearsal for World War II, 38, 77
WPB, powers and procedures of, 40–3, 45, 58–60
WRA, 93

Yakus v. *U. S.,* 44–5, 128–31, 178
Yalta, 137n, 160
Yamashita's case, 121–2

2939

A NOTE ON THE TYPE USED IN THIS BOOK

The text of this book has been set on the Linotype in a type-face called "Baskerville." The face is a facsimile reproduction of types cast from molds made for John Baskerville (1706–1775) from his designs. The punches for the revived Linotype Baskerville were cut under the supervision of the English printer George W. Jones.

John Baskerville's original face was one of the forerunners of the type-style known as "modern face" to printers: a "modern" of the period A.D. *1800.*

The book was composed, printed, and bound by The Plimpton Press, Norwood, Massachusetts.

2939